Eco Hotels of the World

by

Alex Conti

Published by Eco Hotels of the World
PO BOX 563, Macclesfield, Cheshire SK10 9GF, England

Contents

Introduction

Writing this book presented me with difficult, contradictory feelings. I'd be the first to recognise how important travel can be as a cultural tool and as a way to redistribute wealth around the globe, but I also have to admit that it contributes to climate change. So it does seem odd to encourage it. But travel won't cease to exist, so the best I can do is approach it in a way that increases awareness and responsibility about where we go and how we act on holiday. Even the righteously eco-aware can go off their green rails away from home; after all, holidays are when we let loose and have a good time and tend to forget our principles. This book aims to be a guide through the dos and don'ts of eco-travel. It will show you places that have been selected for their eco-awareness in the hope that they will inspire you to make your next holiday greener. You may even take some of their ideas home with you.

Before we get to that I may as well confess. I'm not a hardcore environmentalist. It takes gritty dedication to be that way and I tend to be lazy. I drive a car and have a soft spot for modern technology. But I'm also an unashamed bio-philiac; I love nature and have never lost a child-like wonder about natural world. Some of us start that way and get distracted by work and mortgages until we forget that we ever noticed our environment. Yet most remember, and now that we're older those first impressions of the beauty around us still influence the choices we make.

I trained as an archaeologist. This has little to do with the environment, other than spending most of your time wearing it. My studies took me to great sites all over Europe and it was while studying ancient ways of life that I first noticed how we haven't changed much. As people, we still express the same feelings, still make decisions based on experience and even live in similar social systems. However, there is one huge, gaping difference between us and the ancients. There are far more of us and we are very, very bad at living within our means. We are using up our resources. We expect the impossible from our environment because we've lost touch with nature. We live unaware of what this planet can sustainably provide and what it can't.

Those of us who live in cities and rarely visit the countryside can easily forget how it all works. I have met people who were amazed at seeing fruits on a tree! People who imagined supermarkets had some kind of magic never-ending supply of goods and didn't see a problem with flying food from the other side of the planet to satisfy their whims.

I don't want to go back to tallow candles in a mud hut. I am very comfortable as I am, thanks; I love my computer, my coffee machine and even my TV. But we all need to ask more questions. We need to favour local produce, look after our resources and try living in a more efficient and sustainable way.

Our Rating System

A t first my inspiration was a rating system based on the technical requirements considered by ecologically minded architects. Then, on a cold and windy day in the French countryside while I was staying with friends on an eco-farm, we formulated a list of queries. Armed with these, even before rating a property I'd understand whether the ethos of an hotel (or lodge, camp or villa) was in line with our ideals. To what extent did it complement the natural environment? Was it ecologically sustainable? Did it actively practice conservation? Did it provide environmental training programs? Did it incorporate cultural considerations? Did the local community benefit from it?

These became the questions I consistently asked to define the essence of what makes an eco hotel. Once a property had proven it adhered to most of the above concepts it could be rated. But how? Several star systems rate hotels for comfort but we didn't know of one that rated an hotel's environmental credentials. This book uses a green star system according to five key indicators, which are equally important: energy, water, waste disposal, eco-activity and protection. Of these the last two are not immediately comprehensible, but I'll come to those.

Energy

An average non-eco hotel may have five or six incandescent (traditional) bulbs in each room, and these waste 95% of the energy they use, according to Greenpeace. Greenpeace calculates that phasing them out in the UK alone would save more than five million tonnes in CO_2 emissions a year. Hotels save money when they switch to energy-savers that require infrequent replacement, and the unit costs are dropping all the time but many still do use incandescent ones.

We also consider switches and automatic light-extinguishing systems. Most hotels now have keys that switch lights off when the guest leave a room, and the really big hotels have automated central systems. Smaller lodges and B&Bs rely on staff checks.

The higher-rated hotels have written policies and educate their staff in energy-saving techniques. They invest in energy-efficient appliances and renewable energy sources. Some have solar panels and wind generators. Others use hydro and biomass systems. This can be as easy as switching to a more eco-efficient energy provider , and doesn't have to be expensive.

Water

In the wet wet north, we can easily forget that 54% of Africa' 700 million people don't have reliable access to safe potable water. We merrily flush ours down the lavatory, leave taps running and use expensive drinking water on plants.

Now scale this behaviour up to hotel size and you'll see that places where water is scarce or expensive this can be disastrous. Eco hotels make an effort to conserve water in several ways. Staff are aware of best practice, help to educate guests and update notices in rooms to remind visitors of projects such as towel and linen re-use. Eco hotels of the upper categories install low-flush toilets and low-pressure shower adaptors, build rain-water collectors and recycle grey water on their gardens. Some hotels operate bucket policies – no, not what you think. It's amazing how much more you value water when you know someone's carried it you in a bucket. As to the gardens, we encourage the use of endemic (indigenous) plants, which, being acclimatised, don't usually need any watering at all.

Waste disposal

We can't alter the fact that we leave waste, but we can change how much we produce, how we manage it and finally how we dispose of it. 'Reduce, Re-use, Recycle' is the way of life in most eco hotels. Conscientious eco hoteliers start by keeping down the amount of non-reusable waste coming onto their properties by using local suppliers and asking them to avoid unnecessary packaging.

Some hotels circulate a detailed disposal policy that lets staff and guests know what they're doing and why. Composting organic material is common and kitchen gardens certainly appreciate it. Guests in some hotels can recycle their own waste in separate bins. Elsewhere, especially in remoter resorts, guests may be asked to take plastic litter home to a place where it can be recycled efficiently.

Eco-activity

We believe that an eco hotel's owners should actively protect its environment. Their eco-active rating demonstrates how much they do to raise consciousness. This starts with staff eco-training and spreads to the guests; in many eco hotels you can ask any member of staff about green issues involving the location and they will tell you everything you wish to know. This sometimes turns out to be a free souvenir that visitors take home to make their own lives a little more efficient. Some eco hotels run courses and design new projects from which both the the local community and foreign visitors can learn and benefit.

Protection

The 'environment' isn't just trees and wildlife. It's also the people, their economy and their culture. With this last of the five green star criteria we look at what a hotel is doing for the place and people around it. Hotels can bring welcome foreign income to a town or village, through wages to local staff and good relationships with local suppliers of goods and services.

It's also important to encourage interaction between visitors and the local community. This can start simply enough, by having staff or a local guide take people around and introduce them to the neighbourhood. Some unlikely meetings of cultures prove to benefit both sides; wealthy visitors can find a passion for a local project and invest in it, a specialist engineer can lend free words of encouragement and expertise to a local development, or a villager can demonstrate why tried and tested ways are preferred to the latest technology. The best eco hotels put a lot of effort into conservation programs, local businesses and local staff. They suggest local activities for guests, buy food from the surrounding area and patronise small businesses nearby.

A Simple Look at Climate Change

If you didn't believe that climate change is a reality you probably wouldn't be reading this book. But in the unlikely event that you are not convinced (and I can't attempt in these few pages to change your mind) then all I can say is — living in a more environmentally friendly way is better anyway.

Take cars. Driving less will shrink your carbon footprint and reduce emissions, which is great if you believe man-made global climate change is a fact, and thoroughly unimportant if you don't. But driving less will also make you richer because you won't waste so much on fuel. It'll make you healthier, because you'll walk and cycle more. It will probably, by making you healthier, help you to live longer and who can argue with that?

In the same self-interested vein, I introduce, in my support, The Gambler's Argument, otherwise known as Pascal's Wager. It is derived from the writings of philosopher and mathematician Blaise Pascal (1623-62), who was thinking of something completely different at the time. Uncertain whether or not to be convinced by arguments about the existence of global warming, four possible choices are open to you:

If it is real, you can do something; or not.
If it is not real, again, you can do something; or not.
In this case, if it is not real, you have nothing to lose by doing something (just in case).
But if it is real, you have everything to lose by not doing something.
No contest, really, is there? Extinction of the human race on the one hand, versus a weekend flight to New York to spend money in the overcrowded January sales. Stay at home, perhaps?

Backing environmental projects and environmentally friendly businesses supports an entire industry that works to create and market greener, more sustainable technologies. These improve our lifestyles, our health and our economy. We have nothing to lose and everything to gain.

Some Random Interesting Facts

1 Did you know that one third of all amphibians are dying due to climate change? Climate change has not only triggered and helped spread a fungal skin disease called chytridiomycosis, which is fatal to amphibians, but has also caused habitat loss through weather changes and warming.

2 Did you know that birds, bats, dolphins, antelopes, whales and other migratory creatures are so confused by global warming that they end up in the wrong place at the wrong time to feed and breed? Cranes go to Germany instead of Spain, and can die in a cold snap; whales go where there's no plankton to feed on; and other species may soon find their habitats swamped by rising sea levels, or their forests turned to tundra in the heat.

3 Did you know that global warming has taken a heavy toll on penguins? Reports show that the Antarctic Peninsula's average temperature has risen by 3° to an average −14.7°Celsius (about 6°F) over the past fifty years. Freezing torrential rain, for days on end, is now common. Penguins are born covered in down, warm in snow but soaked through by icy water, so the babies which haven't yet grown water-repellent feathers are getting hypothermia and freezing to death. Adelie penguins could be extinct within ten years.

4 Did you know that rising water temperatures and more intense solar radiation caused by climate change are leading to coral bleaching and disease often resulting in mass coral mortality? Bleaching happens when the water temperature rises to the point where it kills the tiny polyps that make up the coral, leaving behind the white limestone skeleton of the reef. Researchers believe that, should the severity of climate change continue, our 'rainforests of the ocean' could become extinct by the end of this century.

5 Did you know that the sun produces more energy every hour than the entire energy needs of human civilization from the beginning of time?

6 Did you know that electricity from geothermal energy was first produced back in 1904, in Larderello, Italy? Today electricity from geothermal energy is produced in more than twenty countries around the world, accounting for more than 7,000 megawatts of our global electricity provision. Less than 1%, but rising...

7 Did you know that below the earth's surface, temperature increases at a rate of roughly 32°C (90°F) for the first six miles down? This upper six miles of rock under the USA alone contains 6,000 times the geothermal energy of the earth's oil reserves. Trouble is, extracting it. The Romans used geothermally heated water for spa treatments and underfloor heating, and the first North Americans used geothermal energy as far back as 8,000BCE.

Things to Think About... *Before You Go!*

Previous Planning and Preparation Prevents a Poor Performance. This is hardly a sophisticated proposition but one that most of us ignore. Preparation means you'll foresee and prevent problems and spend your precious holiday enjoying yourself rather than worrying about details. Besides, planning is an exciting part of the journey. So:

1 How will I get there and back?
If you have a choice, between for instance road versus rail, or air versus ship, which is the least environmentally harmful? This makes a big difference to the size of carbon footprint that results, to how much you enjoy your holiday and of course, to how much it will ultimately cost.

2 What happens to my money?
Will at least some of your money go to a local community or will most of it go to a big corporation's shareholders or Swiss bank account? If you choose a small eco hotel which uses all the resources locally available to it, you will see the effects in a way you never would at an outpost of a conventional chain.

3 Where am I going?
Invest in a good guidebook and brochures that can be re-used or recycled when you have finished with them. Look on the internet, join travel forums, ask people who have been there and basically do your homework. This can be a lot of fun and saves time at your destination. And even learning the basic foreign-language words for hello, please and thank you will make your stay more pleasant.

4 Will I leave this place as I'd wish to find it?
'Take nothing but photos and leave nothing but footprints' is the eco-traveller's mantra. It's about respect. Try to blend in a bit. If you were to arrive strung about with Nikons and Leicas in the remoter corners of the world where people earn in a year less than your camera is worth, you'd simply look as if you were here to exploit the place. Remember that a display of expensive kit can alienate you from the local community and make you a target for beggars or worse. The locals don't want trouble. If you take pictures of people, please ask permission; they are not just scenery. An exchange of politenesses, even if it's only nods and smiles, helps to create a bond.

5 Will I take the kitchen sink?
Eco hotels rarely demand that you pack a dinner jacket or the family diamonds. Consider what you really must take and what you can buy, should the need arise, at the destination. Over-packing adds a vast dead weight to an airliner's load. This means it uses more fuel and pollutes more. And do you really enjoy humping suitcases the size of motorbikes and backpacks that look as if they conceal an armchair? She who travels light has a better time. Think about all the things you took last time and didn't use or wear. You can wash things, and buy things, when you're there; why take six of everything 'just in case'? And if you do, foolishly, take six of everything – give them away to the chambermaid so you won't have to hump them all the way back.

6 Will I have time to think about my environmental impact?
In the excitement of the moment, on holiday, it'll probably be the last thing on your mind. This is why it's a good idea to plan wisely. Make good decisions in advance. When you feel you have reduced your carbon footprint as far as possible, you can look at offsetting what's left with a carbon offset company you trust. Some of these not only use the money to offset your carbon emissions but also support worthwhile projects in poor areas around the world. Look for one that you like and help them a little on their journey while you look forward to yours.

Things to Think About... *When you are there!*

You go on holiday to enjoy yourself as much as possible away from the worry, care, and mundane concerns of daily life, so it's not surprising if environmental standards slip once you're away from home. Yet what we do goes on having consequences, wherever we are.

1 Your room is your home.
If you wouldn't leave the television or air conditioning on when you're out, or the tap running when you're brushing your teeth, then there is no reason to do it on holiday either. Ignore the tiny mean-minded voice that tells you 'I've paid for it so I'll use it!' because it's pure ecological poison. Some of the newer hotels have card systems to turn everything off, but even so, make sure you haven't inadvertently left something on. Televisions on standby consume an enormous amount of power but a 10-second room check means no resources are wasted whilst you sightsee. To save water and detergent, re-use towels for several days and don't have your bed-linen changed daily. Choose showers in preference to baths. Ask whether plastic from your toiletries can be recycled and if not, take it with you to re-use or recycle at home.

2 Use local knowledge.
Hotel staff should have a good knowledge of the local area. Use them and your guidebook to find things that are off the beaten track. There may be a lot of well-trodden sights to see, but try and combine them with at least one unusual experience and spend your money locally.

3 Transport.
Public transport it is cheaper and usually greener and if you're lucky enough, you may even sit next to somebody interesting. If you do need a car for special excursions, try and find a hire company with a responsibility statement; some even offer hybrids and low-consumption vehicles. You may prefer to rent a pushbike or scooter for most journeys. A bicycle of course is the ultimate eco-transportation device, spinning along at the kind of leisurely speed that is perfect for sight-seeing and helping you to engage with the locals as well as keeping you fit. If the distances are not totally prohibitive and it is safe to do so, most adult travellers can cycle everywhere.

4 Shopping.
Visitors abroad can be a big help to small communities, or they can do outright harm. You only have to think of the trade in endangered animals, and parts such as fur or teeth, supported by some unscrupulous foreign buyers. What we buy on stalls half way around the world is not an inconsequential choice; it can support a cruel business that threatens wildlife. For more information see page 62.

5 In the Sea.
Take simple precautions so that your holiday doesn't affect delicate sea-life like corals. Coral reefs are amongst the most biologically productive and diverse of ecosystems, and directly sustain half a billion people. Careless travellers can make them sicken and die from impact or poisoning. Coral is exceptionally fragile. Do not step on it, or pick any up when swimming or diving. Even kicking sand onto coral can be harmful. As to poisoning, a recent study by the university of Pisa has uncovered the disastrous effect of sun-tan oil and sunscreen on these gentle ecosystems. So please take not to bathe near corals when you're wearing creams or cosmetics of any kind.

Swimming with dolphins is a temptation best resisted. Dolphins are frequently hurt by jewellery that humans bring into the water and they are prone to infections from sun cream. In some areas their welfare takes second place to their earning potential.

6 Animals.
Land animals are vulnerable to uncaring entrepreneurs. It is up to us never to support the cruel exploitation of wild animals that goes on in tourist hotspots. Never give them money and don't have your picture taken with them or take their picture. If you visit sanctuaries or zoos, be conscious of whether or not the creatures are being properly cared for. Ask questions about care and responsibility and make it plain that as a tourist you do not condone ill-treatment.

Choosing a Responsible Tour Operator

Sometimes only an experienced tour operator has the local connections and professional expertise to make a trip possible. Once you've drawn up a short list of possible operators for the trip you want to make, find out whether theirs is a sustainable business model.

Do they keep an eye on environmental issues? Some operators cut carbon emissions by favouring trains rather than planes for internal transfers and hiring only the most energy-efficient buses and cars. Some offer carbon offsetting for their tours or include it in their packages. Other tour operators work from environmentally friendly offices and cut down on paper use by sending electronic brochures and encouraging e-booking and e-ticketing rather than post.

Are they socially responsible?
With the huge old-fashioned traditional tour operators, you may once have suspected that a tiny part of your money trickled down to local businesses while the rest ended up in banks in the Cayman Islands. Specialised operators use local guides, local transport companies and prefer locally owned hotels to large chains.

Are they culturally sensitive?
If the operator you choose knows the destination, they will take you to see the most interesting places with well-informed guides and you won't miss the best events. Your operator should provide a guide who, if not a native speaker, communicates fluently in the local language.
If you use, eat or see the making of traditional products you learn about the culture and resources of a place while assisting its businesses and artisans. If you visit somewhere during a special festival or celebration you find out about

its history. A worthwhile operator will include some local cross-cultural interaction, whether it's to do with food, religion or fashion. Choosing a tour operator is as important as choosing the destination, and if you get it right you'll have a carefree experience with the security that only a good tour operator can provide.

Useful Contacts:

Elevate Destinations
www.elevatedestinations.com
Elevate Destinations designs responsive travel that makes a positive difference. Five percent of the net costs of your trip go to protecting the environment and communities in the countries you visit.

Trusted Adventures, LLC
www.trustedadventures.com
An alliance of industry leaders offering over 350 distinctive trips to more than 100 destinations worldwide.

Diverse Earth
www.diverse-earth.com
For small group tours, family holidays or independent journeys, Diverse Earth specialises in responsible travel for the adventurous explorer.

International Expeditions
www.ietravel.com
International Expeditions specialises in nature travel, taking guests on environmentally responsible expeditions to some of the world's most remarkable places.

Africa

Please note: locations on this map are approximate

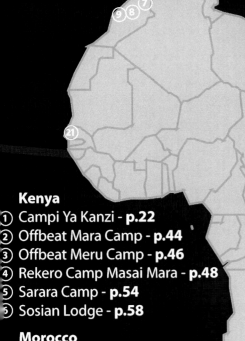

236 Hurumzi Hotel

Tower Top
Restaurant view
of the House of
Wonders

A well-known feature of Zanzibar's skyline, along with minarets, Hindu temple towers, and church spires, is the Tower Top Restaurant at 236 Hurumzi. This hotel, the second tallest building in Stone Town Zanzibar, has been restored to its former opulence as the home of one of the richest men in the Swahili Empire. It is furnished with Zanzibari antiques of varied origins and styles that, together, create an impression of colonial and Arabian Africa.

The 22 guest-rooms are beautiful and romantic, each representing Zanzibari traditions in a distinct way. They have large Zanzibari beds complete with netting, and all but the Kipembe, Livingston and Tipu Tip rooms have large stone bathtubs. Rooms on the lower floors, and the South room, have air conditioning; ceiling fans and the constant breeze keep guests cool on the upper floors. Sultan rooms on the first and second floors have ceilings twenty feet high, carved doors, original stucco décor and hand-painted glass lamps and window panes.

Rooms:
7 suites,
9 standard rooms,
and 6 rooms in the 2
Hurumzi hotel/
residence addition

Facilities:

Two restaurants:
Tower Top Restaurar
and Kidude Café

Jeweler and gift bout
LA OPALA

★ ★ ★

Here at 236 Hurumzi, a close look at the simplest day-to-day work reveals an impressive effort to remain in touch with traditional Tanzanian values and to respect the local environment. Most of the laundry is done by hand and not machine. Fuel lamps are used for emergency night lighting as a traditional alternative to electricity, and although most rooms are equipped with air-conditioners, the staff encourage the use of ceiling fans. Reminders about water and power conservation are displayed in all the guest rooms.

The staff are enthusiastic recyclers and support the use of local products with minimal packaging. The management works to preserve and improve Stone Town via the Rotary Club and other organisations, and participates directly in local government initiatives like the Stone Town Heritage Society.

236 Hurumzi is one of a group of restored mansions built in the 1800s. Dedicated architectural salvage and research has protected the site along with its period furnishings. The management supports key social projects by buying local artefacts (for instance coconut fibre rugs made by the blind) and by donating old sheets and towels to the orphanage. Within the hotel there are great opportunities for the staff who receive in-house and consultant-driven training in new skills including languages and IT. The management lends significant support to its staff and together they have made 236 Hurumzi a pillar of the local community.

236 Hurumzi Hotel has been awarded the Eco Hotels of the World rating of 3 stars.

Brass Bed of the Suite Seyyed

Tower Top Restaurant view of the Indian Temple

The East Room

Address:
P.O Box 3417,
236 Hurumzi Street,
Zanzibar,
Tanzania.

Telephone:
255-24-2232784

Website:
www.236hurumzi.com

E-mail:
236hurumzibookings@zanlink.com

17

Ant's Nest and Ant's Hill

Ant's Nest and Ant's Hill are very special bush homes situated on adjoining private game reserves in the magnificent, malaria free Waterberg (three hours northwest of Johannesburg and a couple of hours south of the Limpopo River). With a guide-to-guest ratio of 1:3, the aim here is to provide a uniquely flexible safari experience offering guests a wide choice of activities to keep everyone entertained, from the youngest to the oldest, from the fittest to those most in need of a rest.

Ant's Nest is hosted by Ant and Tessa Baber and their team. The original homestead, it lies in a natural amphitheatre, with wide verandahs and a classic African atmosphere. The luxurious en-suite rooms accommodate a maximum of twelve guests. Ant's Nest is booked predominantly on an exclusive basis, i.e., to groups of twelve or fewer, although out of high season, you can book just one room.

Ant's Hill was built by Ant and Tessa on the edge of a cliff. This bush home offers breathtaking views across the Waterberg. The draped four-poster beds are seven feet wide and spectacular bathrooms offer sunken baths and waterfall showers. Ant's Hill also caters for a maximum of twelve guests but is usually booked on a non-exclusive basis; however, should you wish to book the entire lodge this can be arranged.

Rooms:
Ant's Nest -
6 bedrooms
Ant's Hill -
5 bedrooms

Ave. Rates:(2008)
R3300.00 p.p.p.n
fully inclusive

Activities:
Horse riding, Gam
drives, Game walk
Mountain biking
Clay pigeon
shooting and mo

Facilities:
Ant's Nest - priva
heated pool,
Mini bar, tea an
coffee. Sandpi
and toys availab
for childres, Bus
gym and volley-
Ant's Hill - mini
and tea and cof
Heated plung
pool overlooki
the gorge. Sanc
and toys for chilc
and a badmint
court.

★ ★ ★

Ant's Nest and Ant's Hill have an acute sense of conservation, as a result of their wild location and because of the know-how of their staff. Electrical appliances and lighting run on battery power and constant monitoring ensures none is used unnecessarily during the day.

Waste is also a primary concern and grey (used) water is fed to a wetland where, once filtered, it water the garden. Showers are recommended rather than baths, cleaning products are biodegradable and linen is changed every two or three days. Solid waste is kept to a minimum as toiletries are not plastic-wrapped, and recycling is carried out throughout the lodges and guest rooms.

The lodges do a lot for the local community too. Supplies are always bought from local traders and suggested activities are in the vicinity where guests can also purchase local crafts.

Ant's Nest and Ant's Hill have been awarded the Eco Hotels of the World rating of 3 stars.

 Address:
PO Box 441,
Vaalwater,0530,
Limpopo,
South Africa

 Telephone:
+27147554296 and +27147553584

 Website:
www.waterberg.net

 E-mail:
reservations@waterberg.net

Bintang Bolong Lodge

The Lodge is in a three-hectare enclosure on the banks of the Bintang Bolong (the largest tributary of the River Gambia), in the middle of a mangrove forest. Visitors experience the exciting flora and fauna of brackish wetlands. As the waters retreat, countless creatures such as crabs and mudskippers are exposed in the sludge of the riverbed. In the evening, apes and vultures inhabit the overhanging baobab trees, and after dusk great colonies of fruit bats can be seen swarming into the night.

A spacious restaurant terrace offers the unique opportunity to watch wildlife in and around the river. As well as flying fish and numerous species of bird, with a little luck you might just catch a glimpse of pelicans and passing dolphins. On this part of the river the tide rises and falls by a metre, so at high tide well over half of the camp is flooded.

Most of the Lodge's accommodation stands on stilts amongst the mangroves, where wooden jetties provide docking facilities. The complex was completely rejuvenated at the end of 2004, and emphasis was put upon traditional building techniques using indigenous materials such as mangrove wood and clay bricks.

Rooms:
14 rooms for
up to 30 guests.

Ave. Rates:
400 GMD p.p.
per night incl.
breakfast.
200 GMD p.p.
for children
under 14.

Attractions:
Crocodile pond
Dance performan
and courses, Dru
courses and
performances
Excursions with
fishermen durir
their daily catc
(also at night)
Experience th
rice and shell
harvest, Excursio
into the anima
and plant
world of Gamb

★★★★

B intang Bolong Lodge's location has forced its staff to be completely self-sufficient. There is no public electricity network so all power is produced by generator, making energy saving a priority.

There is no public water supply either; a well provides water for sanitation. All supplies are bought locally and in bulk to reduce packaging. The Lodge takes recycling and environmental protection seriously and continues to maintain the lowest practicable impact on its delicate surroundings.

The Lodge has been awarded the Eco Hotels of the World rating of 4 stars.

Address:
Foni Bintang Karanai
Western Division
The Gambia.

Telephone:
+220 9929362

Website:
www.bintang-bolong.com

E-mail:
reception@bintang-bolong.com

Campi ya Kanzi

Campi ya Kanzi means Camp of the Hidden Treasure in Kiswahili. The camp lies within a private 400-square-mile Masai estate in Southern Kenya, dominated by Mt Kilimanjaro just 35 miles away. The Masai, as landlords, ensure that it remains one of the last unspoiled areas of Africa. Campi ya Kanzi help the Masai in preserving their wildlife and cultural heritage (Campi ya Kanzi sets aside a daily conservation fee of $100 to assist the Masai community) and in turn you learn about the Masai lifestyle, their land and culture, through them, in the most genuine way.

Campi ya Kanzi accommodates a maximum of 14 guests in six thatched-roof tented cottages and in the Hemingway and Simba suites. The first of these is named after the author who described the nearby Chyulu Hills in Green Hills of Africa, and the other is the Swahili word for 'lion' (Disney fans will of course know that!) Each cottage enjoys a different view, and accommodates one or two adults.

All the cottages are made of stone, fabric and wood and are lit by electricity. Each one has an elegant bath with shower, bidet, basin, hot and cold running water, flush toilet and brass plumbing fixtures to add an unexpected touch of elegance and comfort. The eight cottages are sufficiently far apart to provide privacy. A dedicated Masai attendant is assigned to each one, and at night, askari (night watchmen) patrol the camp.

Rooms:
6 luxury
tented cottages
2 tented suites
1 private house
with room for 1

Ave. Rates:
Price is $650
per person,
inclusive of
$100 conservatio
fee for the Maas
community. Per

All safari activiti
included:
Game drives, Ga
walks, Forest wa
Bird watching
Maasai cultural v
Visits to the
Trust project

The multi-award-winning Campi ya Kanzi demonstrates how a local community and its values can be supported by responsible, sustainable tourism. Despite its remote location, the camp manages to provide all modern conveniences. All electricity is provided by a photovoltaic system, with inverters supplying 220v AC current. Triple-A rated appliances are used throughout the camp to save energy.

Water is the most precious resource here, and the camp has a rainwater collection system. Both grey and black water are recycled through natural filters and used in a wildlife pond. In the same spirit all organic waste is composted and staff are trained to recognise the recycling potential of any material used on camp. Campi ya Kanzi's mission is to protect the environment, its wildlife and Masai culture. The conservation fees, mentioned above, and guests' donations, support the Masai Wilderness Conservation Trust, which employs 115 locals. It promotes conservation, education and health and provides literature, briefings and field experience to guests.

Campi ya Kanzi has been awarded the highest Eco Hotels of the World rating of 5 stars.

Address:
PO Box 236 - 90128,
Mtito Andei,
Kenya.

Telephone:
+254 45 622516
+88 2165 1103557 – Satellite

Website:
www.maasai.com

E-mail:
lucasaf@africaonline.co.ke

Cousine Island

I n this luxury eco-friendly property the owners believe that eco-tourism is not about sitting and watching, but rather that it should involve active and tangible effort. There are just four exclusive villas on Cousine, and no more than ten guests on the island at any time, so human impact is strictly controlled and minimised. Guests enjoy privacy, isolation and a sense of ownership. The Pavilion, with views of the neighbouring islands, features a bar, pool, library, lounge and airy dining area offering delicious food. The Island is also available for exclusive use.

Guests are invited to participate in the conservation work on the island to whatever extent they feel most comfortable. They may wish to plant a tree from the island's nursery of endemic species, or assist the island's ecologists in monitoring critically endangered marine turtles – or simply relax on the beach enjoying the surroundings. Guests always leave Cousine with a much deeper knowledge of environmental issues than they had when they arrived. Even if they choose not to be involved, they are still supporting ongoing conservation and restoration programs by visiting Cousine.

INTRODUCTION

Rooms:
4 Villas

Ave. Rates:
Per night
Euro 1500 plus
7% tax in 2008
Euro 1700 plus
10% tax in 2009

Whole island rental is
available at Euro 5500
plus 7% tax in 2008
and Euro 6500 plus
10% tax in 2009.

Rates include
full board
and all drinks,
except for a
reserve list.

Activities:
Diving
Excursions/Char
Fishing trips
Sailing

★ ★ ★ ★ ★

Cousine Island's aim is to become more carbon efficient and to switch from its present three 60kw generators to solar and wind power. These projects are taking shape and already the water heating system is solar. The staff are conscious of the need to conserve energy, and information on the island's efforts is available to guests. The Island boasts a complex and extensive system of rainwater catching facilities. It can store 350,000 litres of rainwater – enough to take the island through the dry season.

The rainwater is filtered through a UV and sediment filter and is safe for drinking and bathing. The staff are educated in water conservation, and monitor water use constantly; guests can ask for up to date information. Rainwater supplies a small kitchen garden and fills the swimming pool. On an island of this size, waste disposal is also paramount. The staff are well trained in waste management and proper separation of items. They re-use wherever possible, separate organic waste for composting and send the rest to a waste management site in Praslin.

Cousine Island is a special place. Bought for the sole purpose of creating a safe environment for marine turtles to nest in, it has since become a unique project for the preservation of bio-diversity in the Seychelles. A great number of exotic fauna and flora were removed from the island, and indigenous vegetation was replanted on its plateau. Over 5,000 trees were established to create a suitable habitat for the indigenous land birds. Two conservation staff members are permanently employed to monitor and continue the rehabilitation of this fragile environment, helped by numerous guest researchers who ensure this site remains of global natural importance.
Cousine Island has been awarded the highest Eco Hotels of the World 5 star rating.

Address:
P.O. Box 977
Victoria
Mahé
Seychelles

Telephone:
+248 321107

Website:
www.cousineisland.com

E-mail:
cousine@seychelles.net

25

Cousine Island

Cousine Island is the only island in the region with a conservation-based model into which the hotel structure fits. It is recognised nationally and internationally one of the most ecologically important private islands in the world. The island's ecologists are consulted by scientists world-wide on a wide range of ecological and conservation issues. No other private island in the region works at this level, and this is testament to how seriously Cousine's own management treats green issues.

INTRODUCTION

Dar Itrane Ecolodge

D ar Itrane Ecolodge is a mountain hideaway nestling in one of the best preserved valleys in Morocco. It was created to promote a new way of exploring: one that would complement the nature and culture of the High Moroccan Atlas. More than a simple guesthouse, the Ecolodge is concerned with promoting and protecting Berber culture.

It is an ideal base for nature tourism, walking in the villages, hiking and trekking in the surrounding mountains. It offers seventeen double rooms with private bathrooms, roof terraces and patios. There is a hammam and plenty of communal space, including a library and two lounges. The Ecolodge is also a great place to taste traditional but sophisticated Moroccan cooking.

Dar Itrane - Interior yard

Rooms: 17
All en-suite

Ave. Price: 40 €
p.p. half board

Hotel facilitie

Hammam
Common room
2 living room
Library
Landline at
reception
Dining room

★ ★ ★ ★

Dar Itrane Ecolodge subtly educates guests in the importance of saving energy and water. The staff recognise ways to save these precious resources and actively encourage guests to re-use room linens and to conserve water and electricity (although an automatic light-extinguishing system is in place in case of forgetfulness). An active investment program will provide a solar heating plant and modern double-glazing and insulation.

Terrace view over the mountain range M'Goun

Waste is carefully separated on site. Staff at Dar Itrane have got so good at recycling that the whole town relies on their expertise; there is now a training scheme, aimed at local children, which is helping to create a new generation of environmentally aware people. The staff can willingly advise guests on eco schemes and an ethical traveller's charter is in every room. Part of the hotel revenue is devoted to a 'Your participation, our commitment' program created by Dar Itrane to help Berber projects. Berber culture is very important here and you will find plenty of information in the Ecolodge including books, videos and music in the library, as well as walking and hiking itineraries to guide you through fascinating villages and allow you to meet their friendly inhabitants.

Twin bed room

Dar Itrane Ecolodge has been awarded the Eco Hotels of the World rating of 4 stars.

Address:
Imelghas village,
Bougmez Valley,
Tabant community,
Azilal district,
Morocco

Telephone:
+33 (0)4 72 53 72 19 (booking in France)
+212 (0)23 459 312 (landline in Dar Itrane)

Website:
www.dar-itrane.com

E-mail:
sejour@origins-lodge.com

Terrace in the evening

Fumba Beach Lodge

Fumba Beach Lodge, located on the remote south-west of Zanzibar island within the Menia Bay Conservation Area, is a luxury lodge with 26 rooms, a restaurant, a lounge area, a pool and a PADI dive centre offering diving, snorkelling, kayaking and wind surfing. Within the property there is also a spa, with traditional Zanzibari treatments, and a Jacuzzi built on top of a huge African baobab tree; the ideal place to sip a sun-downer with your loved one.

The Lodge is located on forty acres of private land and has a beautiful coastline full of hidden sandy coves where you can relax, take a swim and enjoy the views over the Indian Ocean in total privacy. Most of the twenty deluxe rooms are built overlooking the ocean and are all en-suite. They come in two categories. Luxury suites are right on the beach with outside double shower, a bath overlooking the ocean, a front terrace and a rooftop terrace. Baobab suites are built around a huge Baobab tree, right on the ocean, with a unique outside bath nestled against the big tree.

Rooms: 26

Ave. Rates:
On Request

Activities:
Rest & Relaxati
Scuba Diving
Dolphin Tour
Historic Stone T
Jozani Fores
Spice Tour

F umba Beach Lodge enjoys a perfect location immersed in nature and next to the Indian Ocean. This location brings also particular responsibility to the staff and management of the lodge who have been specially trained in the need to conserve energy and water. They are aware of power and water wastage and avoid using chemicals in their housekeeping. Within the property there is an advanced system of waste disposal, which includes waste separation, a small incinerator, and composting.

The hotel also co-operates with various organisations including the WWF and the Menia Bay Conservation Area. The PADI dive centre participates in marine conservation projects and education, and staff organise beach-cleaning days, remove fishing nets from coral reefs and deter poachers. Lodge staff are locals, and 55% of them come from Fumba village.

Fumba Beach Lodge has been awarded the Eco Hotels of the World rating of 3 stars.

Address:
Po Box 3705
Zanzibar.
Tanzania

Telephone:
+255-(0) 777 876298

Website:
www.fumbabeachlodge.com

E-mail:
info@fumbabeachlodge.com

Guludo Beach Lodge

S queezed between the extraordinary Indian Ocean and wild African bush, Guludo Beach Lodge overlooks one of the most beautiful beaches in Mozambique. In the north of the Quirimbas National Park, Guludo offers access to spectactular wildlife, both above and below the ocean. From here you can discover local wonders, dive coral reefs, explore nearby islands, trek through some of the vast African bush and all the while, soak up a rich culture which takes pride in the hospitality of its people.

Guludo has been built according to strict ethical principles, so that both the host community and the environment receive maximum benefit. It has recently won an award for its innovative design, which emerged from local architectural styles and uses exclusively local materials to guarantee the slightest possible environmental impact. You can stay in a tent or a banda. The award-winning tents are stylishly furnished; you feel you're outside but have the comfort of being inside. The new eco-friendly bandas are Swahili-inspired high roof shelters with spacious verandahs and breathtaking views.

Rooms:
9 sea-facing
rooms in total
composed of:
new bandas,
tented bandas
and a family/
honeymoon sui

Ave Rates:
Standard rate
2008 $255-27.
2009 $295 – 33

Activities:
Skuba diving
Snorkelling,
Whale watchin
Mangroves,
Village footba
Village visit,
Island visits,
Sunset dhov
cruises.

The design of Guludo Beach Lodge minimises energy use at all levels. Thick mud walls with lime render create passive cooling; high roofs maximise air flow, so there is no need for fans or air conditioning. Light is from paraffin lamps, soon to be replaced with solar. The kitchen and bar use gas, and the office runs on a mixture of solar power and a small, efficient generator.

Water use is kept low in the most natural way. Since all water is carried by hand to the rooms, guests are encouraged to be thrifty with it. Grey water is collected for gardening. Recycling also has a very guest-oriented approach. Guests are asked to take any plastic packaging home with them (within reason) and the Lodge's purchasing policy means minimal packaging is bought. Waste is either recycled, used for compost or taken to Pemba City for disposal.

The Lodge is directly involved in a number of conservation projects. Marine biologists are employed to run and implement projects from here, including the coral reef and humpback whale surveys. Over 5% of income from the lodge goes directly to community and conservation projects. Local businesses are also supported and guests are encouraged to visit the local entrepreneurs. The Lodge makes a conscious effort to use local suppliers who sell their fruit, vegetables, seafood, eggs and other produce to the kitchens, much of the time at higher cost than if bought in the nearby town.

Guludo Beach Lodge has been awarded the highest Eco Hotels of the World rating of 5 stars.

Address:
Guludo Quirimbas National Park
Cabo Delgado
Mozambique

Telephone:
00 501 662 4475
0044 (0) 207 127 4727

Website:
www.guludo.com

E-mail:
contact@bespokeexperience.com

Hog Hollow Country Lodge

In 1993, what was to become Hog Hollow Country Lodge was an alien wattle plantation set in the semi-wilderness of a little known area called The Crags. Years before, farmers had been encouraged to do away with the rare, indigenous forest and fynbos (shrubs) which grow only in this small Tsitsikamma area, to plant a fast-growing, invasive and strangling species of Australian wattle for use as tannin and pulp for the leather industry. Andy Fermor, after a six-year sojourn in England and south-east Asia, decided to use his skills and energy to invest in the fledgling democracy of the new South Africa. With scant financial backing but lots of enthusiasm, what started out as a dream has become a beautiful 16-suite reality.

As Hog Hollow rose from the wattle wasteland, Debbie Reyneke was considering her options. Years of hard work had put her at the top of the hotel industry, but always at the back of her mind was the dream of creating something within tourism that would be more meaningful and involving. A great walker and enthusiastic lover of nature, Debbie invited a friend to walk the Otter Trail – a five-day trail along the wild coastal edge of the Tsitsikamma National Park. Tired and hungry at the end of a successful walk, her friend suggested they have dinner in a newly created lodge she'd heard about, built on the edge of a gorge ~ a place called Hog Hollow. That's when Debbie met Andy ... and the rest, as they say, is history.

Rooms: 16

Rate:
from R1276
pppn B & B

In-room facilities
Ceiling fans/
fireplace/heaters
mini-bar/ mini-hi-
tea & coffee static
hairdryer/ safe/toile

In main house facil
Complimentary inte
wireless connecti
telephones/swimr
pool/sauna/
honesty bar at
swimming poo
breakfast,lunch & c
served/library/bar
Children welcor
No Television

★★★

This year Hog Hollow Country Lodge was one of the first six properties in South Africa to receive the coveted Wilderness Foundation Green Leaf award, which seeks to ensure that properties like Hog Hollow are audited and assessed for their environmental management and skills. The staff are strongly aware of energy saving techniques and the lodge is going through some improvements to include a centralised lighting system.

Water saving facilities are very impressive with a total rain water capture capacity of 200,000 litres and water saving systems in every guest shower and toilet cistern. The Lodge also helps to safeguard the local environment by maintaining a watch on endemic plants. In its nine hectares, an interesting de-wattling project aims to eradicate the alien wattle plantations and allow the local indigenous forest to remain strong.

Waste disposal is taken seriously and the Lodge works on educating the neighbourhood in the advantages of recycling, besides being involved in other local community projects. One special initiative is Kids of Kurland, which provides funding for an extra teacher at the local school, in which overcrowding can be a problem. Furthermore Hog Hollow has been accredited as Fair Trade (the 13th such property in South Africa). There is a constant effort to ensure that local employees are fairly treated and to improve their working and living conditions. The Lodge continues to provide stability and hope in a region often spoiled by poverty. Hog Hollow Country Lodge has been awarded the Eco Hotels of the World rating of 3 stars.

Address:
PO Box 503 Plettenberg Bay 6600 (postal)
Askop Road, The Crags, 6602 (physical)

Telephone:
+27 (0) 44 534 8879

Website:
www.hog-hollow.com

E-mail:
info@hog-hollow.com

Ibo Island Lodge, Quirimbas Archipelago

Ibo is just one of a string of 32 tropical islands that make up the breathtakingly beautiful Quirimbas Archipelago in Northern Mozambique. Here you can stroll along empty beaches and explore some of the world's richest coral reefs. If you have sea legs, you can sail a coastline fringed by tropical islands on an Arab dhow - still built to the same design as the vessels which sailed from Indiaa thousand years ago. Snack on cashew nuts and tropical fruit and dine on the freshest seafood of every description.

Guests are spoilt for choice when it comes to finding things to do. They have a rare chance to interact with wonderfully hospitable islanders who are proud to show off their culture and customs. The Lodge consists of three magnificent mansions: Villas Paradiso, Niassa and Bela Vista. All are over a hundred years old, with walls over a metre thick and lofty ceilings.

Accommodation is in Paradiso and Niassa; Bela Vista is the public area and houses the Lodge's restaurant and shop and the main pool in the large garden. All bedrooms are individually designed and unique, with many opening onto private verandahs, bedecked with hand-crafted furniture and soft cushions covered in vibrant local fabrics.

Rooms: 14

Ave. Rates:
Low Season:
US$295 per
person sharin

Activities:
Historical &
Cultural
Island tours
Kayaking int
the mangro
forest, Bird
watching,
Dhow safari
Private san
bank beach
Traditiona
Ibo massag

I bo Island Lodge takes a pride in being able to offer luxury accommodation in an ecologically aware manner. This is something it does very well. Electricity is available during certain hours of the day only, and comes from high-tech generators with a capacity that varies according to occupancy. Run-off from showers and drains is directed to a collection area where water is re-used for irrigation. All Lodge drinking water is filtered rainwater. Sound watering practices (with most garden watering taking place at night with recycled water) plus the use of indigenous plants have created a very efficient and beautiful garden for guests to enjoy.

Recycling is important here. Paper and glass are taken to a facility in Pemba for sorting whilst organic material is used to compost the vegetable garden. The guest check-in procedure details guidelines on responsible tourism on Ibo and, just in case, the staff are well trained in all environmental aspects of the property. Tourism awareness training is an essential component of the community training initiatives they undertake in order to reduce the impact of tourism in these beautiful surroundings. The Lodge has had a noticeably positive impact on local society. It employs thirty permanent staff and a further twenty extended-family members rely indirectly on the business.

Ibo Island Lodge has an important place in the island community, so it is imperative that its operations continue in the most responsible way. Ibo Island Lodge is also involved in a number of projects affecting every aspect of life in the area, from agriculture to training and trade oriented schemes that benefit every inhabitant of this paradise island. Ibo Island Lodge has been awarded the Eco Hotels of the World rating of 3 stars.

Address:
Head Office and Central Reservations:
Suite C6,
Westlake Square,
7966 Cape Town,
South Africa

Telephone:
+27 21 702 0285

Website:
www.iboisland.com

E-mail:
info@iboisland.com

Kurisa Moya Nature Lodge

Kurisa Moya is a beautiful nature lodge in the Northern (Limpopo) Province of South Africa. This haven nestles in the northern Drakensberg escarpment and overlooks the breathtaking Kudu River valley. It is only 45 minutes from the city of Pietersburg (Polokwane) and twenty minutes from the village of Haenertsburg and the steep mountain pass of Magoebaskloof.

Kurisa Moya, meaning Tranquil Spirit, enjoys a strategic position that blesses it with temperate weather which nurtures a beautiful indigenous forest where a large variety of birds, animals and flora can be seen. Large stretches of forest give way to African bush-veld on the lower part of the farm where two dams are fed by clean mountain streams.

Activities at Kurisa Moya include bird-watching, hiking and trout fishing in the dams, where otters and water birds can also be seen. Samango monkeys, baboons, bushbuck, bushbabies, vervet monkeys, warthogs and bushpigs are often seen or heard on the hiking trails. Besides the trails, Ben and Lisa offer cranio-sacral therapy, guided bird walks, fly-fishing lessons, abseiling, mountain biking and back massages... to name but a few.

Rooms:
Farmhouse -
5 rooms,
1 Cabin with
loft rooms,
1 Cottage with
loft rooms.

Ave. Rates:
R400.00 pppn
self catering
(2008)
Kids half-price.
R450.00 pppn
self catering
(2009)

Facilities/Activit*
Birdlife SA
accredited Guid
Guided birdin
outings, Guide
nature walks,
marked walkin
trails, Hiking,
Abseiling,
Sunset 4x4 dri
Massages,
Fly-fishing lesso
Cultural tour
Village home-s*

★ ★ ★ ★ ★

Kurisa Moya has a stalwart attitude towards energy conservation. The property is completely electricity-free; computers run on solar power and main appliances on gas. Staff are trained in operating in an electricity-free environment. They encourage minimum water usage, with linen re-use programmes and grey water recycling which helps to maintain the beautiful gardens.

The Farmhouse, with its mountain and indigenous forest setting, is perfect for bigger groups.

Kurisa Moya has a fine-tuned educational aspect. Staff are encouraged and trained to act in an environmentally responsible way. There is a healthy partnership with rural schools in the area, and guests can donate items and get involved in the schools' upkeep if they wish. Staff work extensively in other local eco-projects and even run their own carbon-offsetting scheme through which guests can plant trees at schools and clinics. They also run guided nature walks and promote village home-stays.

This love for local life informs their business relationships too and Kurisa Moya encourages guests to visit local artisans and artists, whilst insisting on the use of local suppliers for their own provisions. There is plenty of literature on all the activities undertaken in the property and a comprehensive, written eco-constitution. Kurisa Moya has been awarded the highest Eco Hotels of the World rating of 5 stars.

Kurisa Moya's Forest Lodge Cabins are 3 metres up in the indigenous forest canopy.

Address:
P O Box 280,
Haenertsburg, 0730
Limpopo,
South Africa

Telephone:
+27 (0) 15 276 1131
+27 (0) 82 200 4596

Website:
www.krm.co.za

E-mail:
info@krm.co.za

Nkwichi Lodge

Mozambique has made a remarkable recovery over the last few years by becoming one of Africa's up and coming tourist destinations. One of its highlights is Lake Niassa (Lake Malawi). Nkwichi Lodge is located on the eastern shores of this stunning lake. The lodge has played an important part in Mozambique's renaissance, acting as a shining light for responsible tourism.

First impressions are so important. There are no roads within ten miles of Nkwichi; you can only reach the Lodge by boat. This immediately creates a feeling of remoteness and tranquillity. You hardly notice the lodge as you arrive on the sandy beach, so well does it blend in with the surrounding scenery. However, you will immediately notice the warm welcome given to you by the local Nyanja people. They are there to ensure you have a memorable stay at Nkwichi. It's up to you how much or how little you do here. The lake is the perfect setting in which to swim, snorkel, sail or canoe whilst the Manda Community Game Reserve is all around for you to explore, walk and visit local communities. However much exercise you take, there is always the comforting knowledge that you can return to the white sandy beach, relax, sunbathe and read a good book.

Rooms:
7 Chalets
2 Houses

Ave. Price:
US$ 240
p.p.p.n. based
on 2 adults
sharing.

Facilities:
En-suite with
al fresco
bathrooms.
All chalets
have their
own private
dining area
Safes are
provided in
the rooms

★ ★ ★ ★ ★

Nkwichi Lodge is entirely run on solar power. All grey water is sand-filtered before it irrigates the surrounding vegetation, which in turn attracts a great number of birds and wildlife. Recycling is extensive. Food waste becomes compost, which is used on the farm, which grows organic vegetables for the Lodge, and trains local farmers in sustainable farming practices.

Glass bottles are cut in half and sanded down into drinking tumblers; the remainder of the glass is used as an alternative to sandpaper by the carpentry department. Tin cans are turned into graters to help women break down the cassava crop before laying it out to dry.

By introducing tourism to the area. the Lodge is working towards providing many local people with an alternative to the subsistence farming and fishing they currently rely on, either through direct employment or by producing the food and supplies the Lodge needs. Each chalet has printed folders giving cultural, historical, social and environmental information on the area. There are introductory talks, guided walks and chats around the fire to complete the 'learning' aspect of a special stay in an unforgettable and pristine corner of the world.

Nkwichi Lodge has been awarded the highest Eco Hotels of the World rating of 5 stars.

 Address:
CP123 Lichinga,
Niassa Province,
Mozambique.

 Telephone:
none

 Website:
www.mandawilderness.org

 E-mail:
mdw01@bushmail.net

Eco Lives

In 1996 five friends, all with a pioneering spirit and a passion for Africa, embarked on a mission to build a new safari lodge in Mozambique. Their dream was to provide guests with beautiful accommodation from which they could explore the surrounding wilderness and communities. They wanted to ensure the protection of local wildlife and provide social and economic benefits for local people. That dream is now a reality and Nkwichi lodge continues to provide excellent accommodation in the heart of wild Mozambique whilst supporting The Manda Wilderness Community Trust. The Trust ensures that local communities benefit from the growth of responsible tourism in the region and manages the Manda Wilderness Game Reserve, which was created to protect and administer a 100,000-hectare community reserve on the shores of Lake Niassa.

Nkwichi has an impressive garden project. Local farmers have learnt how to grow fresh fruit, vegetables and other food to supply the Lodge with delicious produce every day. Its chefs use their imagination and skills to provide a mixture of western recipes along with more traditional African food - all cooked in solar powered ovens!

Offbeat Mara Camp

Dining at night

O ffbeat Mara Camp is a seasonal camp located on the Olare Orok river on Koyiaki Group Ranch. This small and exclusive tented camp offers a private, traditional safari experience with access to the famous Masai Mara Game Reserve.

Tucked away in a prime wildlife area, Offbeat Mara Camp provides guests with superb game viewing – lion, leopard, elephant and buffalo are all seen regularly. Most importantly, the Camp is far from other lodges and camps. The aim is to provide guests with great game viewing 'away from the masses'.

The Masai Mara plays host to the annual migration from July to September. An enormous concentration of wildebeeste, zebra and, consequently, predators, pass through the surrounding plains. Unrestricted by game reserve rules around the Camp, guests can enjoy daytime game drives as well as night drives in custom-built Land Cruisers, bush breakfasts, picnics and sundowners. Guests also have full access to the Game Reserve, the Mara River and early morning balloon trips.

The Camp sleeps twelve guests in six large tents - three doubles and three twins. (An extra bed can be added to each one, for small children). The spacious tents have en-suite bathrooms with hot bucket showers, wash basins and flush loos. They are all furnished with large, handmade cedar beds, 24-hour solar lighting and the finest linen.

Rooms:
6 tents
(12 beds)

Ave. Rates:
Approx. $450
per adult
(all inclusive

Facilities:
Sitting room
library, solar
power

Activities:
Game drives
cultural visit
sundowner

T he Offbeat Mara camp is run in perfect harmony with its environment. Its small size means that there is no impact on local landscape and that the water usage is minimal. Guests have a shower allowance and all other needs are fulfilled by rainwater.

Power in the camp is solar, the kitchen runs on gas and there is a small generator for backup. The social involvement of the camp is also of great interest as there is a close working relationship with the local Masai community. Local Masai even helped build the camp with Piers Winkworth, the owner and head guide at Offbeat Mara Camp. Several of them are now working as camp staff and guides.

The Camp has been awarded the Eco Hotels of the World rating of 4 stars.

Photos from left to right:
Library and sitting room
Secluded accommodation
Masai warrior

Address:
Po Box 1146,
Nanyuki 10400,
Kenya.

Telephone:
+254 (0) 62 31081

Website:
www.offbeatsafaris.com

E-mail:
bookings@offbeatsafaris.com

45

Offbeat Meru Camp

This small, traditional camp is on the edge of the Meru National Park in the Bisanadi National Reserve, an area almost brought to its knees in the 1980s and 1990s by heavy poaching, but now once again home to the Big Five animals of Africa (including the recently re-introduced rhino) – as well as many other species such as Grevy's zebra, reticulated giraffe, leopard, gerenuk and lesser kudu.

The Park has thirteen rivers running through it, which encourage a spectacular variety of birdlife. It was immortalised by Joy Adamson in Born Free, and since it has only two Lodges, the likelihood of seeing anyone else while you stay here is small. You feel you have it to yourself.

The Camp has only six tents: three twin, three double, each one furnished with a large iron bed, its own en-suite bathroom, traditional bucket shower and flushing loo. This area of Kenya gets quite hot during the dry season. After an active morning in the bush there's no better feeling than coming back to camp and cooling off in the stunning infinity swimming pool, watching the wildlife as it comes to drink from the Bisanadi River below you.

Pool and sitting
dining tent

Rooms:
6 tents (12 bed

Ave. Rates:
Approx. $350
per adult
(all inclusive

Facilities:
Swimming po
sitting room
library,
solar powe

Activities:
Game drive
walking, fishi
bush breakfa
sundowner

46

★ ★ ★ ★

Tents at the Offbeat Meru Camp have 24-hour solar lighting, while the rest of the camp is lit by traditional Tilley lamps. Informal dining is hosted in the mess tent or around the campfire. The mess tent has comfortable sofas, a writing table and bar.

Water conservation features include careful storage and retention of rainwater for cooking and laundry. Waste is kept to an absolute minimum and the camp is proud to have no impact on the delicate environment in which it is placed.

The Camp has been awarded the Eco Hotels of the World rating of 4 stars.

Cool spacious tents

Bisanadi River

Address:
Po Box 1146,
Nanyuki 10400,
Kenya.

Telephone:
+254 (0) 62 31081

Website:
www.offbeatsafaris.com

E-mail:
bookings@offbeatsafaris.com

Rekero Camp Masai Mara

S et amidst the teeming wildlife of the Masai Mara area, more precisely directly within the game reserve, the Rekero's tented camp is very close to where the Mara and Talek rivers meet. The camp is ideally situated for the annual migration of over one million wildebeeste and 200,000 zebra from the Serengeti through to the Masai Mara in Kenya and will allow you to not only witness the majestic sight but also to enjoy the hospitality of the Beaton family who, from 1946, have been at the forefront of conservation in this region.

The Camp is set up seasonally (June to October and December to March). It can cater for 18 guests. Gerard and Rainee Beaton, along with their partner Jackson Ole Looseyia, own and host this unique place. Their team of professional Masai safari guides and camp crew have worked together for years, providing guests with an in-depth and memorable Masai Mara experience, including a unique insight into the wildlife, culture, flora and fauna.

Rooms:
8 Tents
Maximum of
18 people
in camp

Ave. Rates:
$600 per
person per nig
approximatel

List of Acitivitie
Guided Gam
Drives, Walkin
Cultural Villag
Visits,
Sundowner
Pic-nic breakfa
or lunch.

★ ★ ★

The Rekero Camp Masai Mara is a tented camp that runs on solar power. This is used to feed a number of energy-efficient low-wattage bulbs and is supplemented by a generator that runs for a maximum of four hours a day and helps maintain the energy-efficient fridges and freezers at a perfect temperature.

Water conservation is also an important aspect of this project and guests use bucket showers, reducing the possibility of water wastage. None of the tents has running water so usage is kept naturally low.

With a tented camp, waste disposal is an ever-present issue. All waste is disposed of offsite and separated, glass and plastic being recycled in order to keep land-fill to a bare minimum. The camp is set up as a charity, and guests are able to donate to one of the many projects that the Rekero is involved in.

Whenever possible the camp helps to promote local businesses and it always buys local produce. Over 90% of the staff are locals, and have been for the past twenty years.

Rekero Camp Masai Mara has been awarded the Eco Hotels of the World rating of 3 stars.

Address:
PO Box 56923,
Nairobi 00200
Kenya

Telephone:
+ 254 721 486272

Website:
http://rekero.com/

E-mail:
rekerocamp@africaonline.co.ke

Roses Camp

The eco-friendly Roses camp, run by the French company Origins and set in the lush Roses Valley of the South Atlas region, is both traditional in its architecture and progressive in its concept. Surrounded by fields of wheat and barley, roses, peaches and melons for most of the year, the eco-camp provides guests with a traditional Berber-style accommodation in five large comfortable Caidal tents. Everything about the tent encampment is made to measure locally and forms an almost seamless natural addition to the environment.

This magnificent riverside setting close to the Dades valley is the ideal base for a trek through the valley along the riverbanks, through fields of roses, past rammed-earth Kasbahs and houses or into the mountains. A large central tent serves as a dining room and living room, where tea and other drinks are provided. You will also find a steamer trunk transformed into a special tiny library devoted to the desert and Berber culture.

Rooms:
Tent-rooms: 5

Ave. Rates:
50 Euros

Facilities:
1 common ter
including a
library box,
sanitary tent
with 2 toilets
and 2 showe
Activities:
Trekking,
Short walks
Paid service
Guided tour
with a loca
guide, Renti
mules and c

Due to its setting in the middle of wheat fields, you will only find candles and lanterns for light; there is no mains electricity. Given this location, donkeys provide most of the transport, and motor taxis are usually hired communally.

The staff is very attentive to water and disposal policies and the use of hot water is limited. Waste separation is also extensively carried out on camp and the efficiency of the on-site staff has helped to teach the local population the advantages of good practice. In each room guests will find a copy of the ethical traveller's charter and part of the night's takings (3€ per person per night) is taken and distributed via the 'Your participation, our commitment' program to local development projects.

The Roses camp is a kind of pilot project for the area and needed special authorisation by the local authorities. The idea was to develop an environmentally friendly accommodation that would bring prosperity to the valley and a new source of revenue to the local communities. To that extent it has already been a huge success. The staff are all from the local community and only local products are used in the camp's day-to-day running. Furthermore guests can experience a real Berber experience by taking advantage of one of the many special ties the camp enjoys with local families. Great walking and hiking itineraries are possible in the vicinity and the camp guides are only too happy to assist with special tours.

Roses Camp has been awarded the Eco Hotels of the World rating of 3 stars.

Address:
Garden of Agoulzi,
Taberkhachte village,
Ouarzazate district,
Morocco

Telephone:
+33 (0)4 72 53 72 19 (booking in France)

Website:
www.origins-lodge.com

E-mail:
sejour@origins-lodge.com

Saharan Camp Atta

The Atta Camp is a luxury desert camp perfect for escaping the hustle and bustle of city life. Set in the impressive Tassilis landscape, close to the nomad village of Remlia, this Saharan camp provides intimacy for private groups or for honeymooners looking for something different in Morocco. The setting is idyllic and you will find ample opportunity to take in great views of one of the most remote areas of the country.

Guests stay in traditional nomad tents, renovated and transformed into comfortable double rooms. After a walking tour or an excursion, the desert camp provides all the comforts including hot showers and traditional Moroccan tajine dinners under the stars – rare luxuries in the middle of the Moroccan desert.

Tent-Rooms: 1
Average price: 5

Camp facilitie
1 common ter
including an
ancient chest lib
2 toilet tents,
2 shower ten

★★★

This camp stands in the Sahara so water efficiency is absolutely paramount. Policies such as hot water rationing and a towel and linen re-use program ensure there is no wastage in an area that demands an eagle eye on consumption. For similar reasons, there is no electricity; the camp relies on lamps and candles. The staff are sensitive to disposal issues and have implemented an efficient waste separation policy: organic waste is given to the goats, and paper and card waste becomes fuel for local bread ovens. Other waste is separated and taken to the nearest recycling centre in Ouarzazate.

Every tent has ample information on eco-living and responsible travelling. Staff are able to advise on all aspects of green living, drawing upon their knowledge of traditional nomadic life. The tents built here are identical to those used by the Ait Atta tribes, made with goat hair – only in this case finished with all the modern comforts. Each day on camp is full of discovery, on foot or in all-terrain vehicles, learning about nomadic life and enjoying views over the wonderful dunes.

Saharan Camp Atta has been awarded the Eco Hotels of the World rating of 3 stars.

 Address:
Remlia village
Er Rachidia province,
Morocco

 Telephone:
+33 (0)4 72 53 72 19 (booking in France)

 Website:
www.origins-lodge.com

 E-mail:
sejour@origins-lodge.com

Sarara Camp

The Namunyak Wildlife Conservation Trust, an area of approximately 75,000 hectares, lies folded around the southern corner of the Matthews mountain range of northern Kenya, home to the proud Samburu tribespeople. The Trust was set up in 1995 specifically to promote wildlife conservation and to assist the local community to benefit from tourism, in return for protecting the wildlife species living on their land.

The conservation work carried out by the Namunyak Trust to date has been hugely successful. Today, several thousand elephant arc living and breeding peacefully in the southern Matthews Range area, together with other wildlife species such as buffalo, lion, leopard, cheetah, African wild dog, greater and lesser kudu, gerenuk, reticulated giraffe, impala and dik dik.

Accommodation at Sarara Camp is in five double tents, each with flush loos and open-air showers. A natural rock swimming pool overlooks a waterhole that is frequently visited by animals. The main lounge and dining area are on a wooden deck with commanding views of the northern frontier.

Rooms:
5 tents

Ave. Price:
US$ 515 + US$
conservancy fe
Prices per perso
sharing per nig

Facilities:
Pool
Mess Area

★ ★ ★ ★

Sarara Camp is an excellent example of man living in harmony with nature. Every electrical item is powered by the sun and the staff have a highly tuned sense of energy conservation which has led to innovations like a power-free cold room for storing fresh fruit and vegetables. Water is also a precious commodity and luckily the camp enjoys the use of a natural fresh-water spring, which also feeds the pool and eventually, even the elephants' waterhole.

Used packaging is kept to an absolute minimum and whatever is left over is offered to the local Samburu as a sort of social recycling. Of course the Samburu own the camp and help run it. Guests are not only able to learn from their fascinating culture but are encouraged to assist in projects which benefit the local people.

The ethos of this camp is not only to help the Samburu (the camp brings them an income) but also to show appreciation for the wilderness and culture here. Guests are able to learn so much, and enjoy unique sights like the 'singing well' or the nearest manyatta where some of the community live. When you couple this with the incredible natural beauty of the area and the teeming wildlife, its hard to think of a better place to enjoy Africa.

Sarara Camp has been awarded the Eco Hotels of the World rating of 4 stars.

Address:
Namunyak Wildlife Conservation Trust
P O Box 30907
Nairobi 00100
Kenya

Telephone:
+254 (0)733614705

Website:
www.bush-and-beyond.com

E-mail:
info@bush-and-beyond.com

Lakeside
swimming pool

Shiluvari Lakeside Lodge

S et against a backdrop of mountains, forests, holy lakes and sacred ruins, Shiluvari is a great place to explore the heart of ancient Venda and restore your natural rhythm. On a natural peninsula amid thirty hectares of natural vegetation, Shiluvari, with its sweeping views of the Albasini Dam and Luonde Mountains, is a perfect base for exploring this land of legend.

The main Lodge, once the old farmhouse, houses the award winning Wood-Owl country restaurant, the Hog and Hound bar and fireplace, the Textures art outlet, a wraparound terrace for alfresco dining, and the reception area. Facilities also include the Lakeside swimming pool and a motorised raft, the Savannah, for sunset cruises along the Luvuvhu river.

Shiluvari lodge has accommodation for everyone. There are standard rooms, thatched chalets and even a family suite, the Mukhondeni. All offer seclusion and privacy with high quality furniture and fittings, including remarkable local art which can be bought in the villages.

Rooms: 14
8 standard
6 thatched
cottages and
a Mukhondeni
Suite (2 rooms

Ave. Price:
From R450 p.
per night
including
breakfast

★★★★

Shiluvari Lakeside Lodge is visibly rooted in the community, from the local art on the walls of its rooms to its less noticeable, but important, policy of buying only from local suppliers.

Hog & Hound pub and lounge

Accredited by Fair Trade and Tourism South Africa, the lodge is involved in several initiatives related to conservation and green tourism. Efficiency is guaranteed by choosing energy saving equipment and lighting. Water is pumped from the Lodge's borehole and and supplemented with rainwater collected from the roof. Showers are preferred in room installations, and there is a drive to install solar panels for hot water.

Typical en-suite bedroom

A project is in place to eradicate invasive alien species of bluegum, eucyluptus and lantana and to ensure the proliferation of endemic plants. But nothing is wasted, and invader wood is used in the excellent hotel furniture. In the same spirit of re-use, disposal is taken seriously and there is a healthy policy of separation.

Shiluvari Lakeside Lodge has been awarded the Eco Hotels of the World rating of 4 stars.

local artwork in bathroom

Address:
Po Box 560, Louis Trichardt, 0920.
Shiluvari Lakeside Lodge
Albasini Dam, Elim
Louis Trichardt
Limpopo Province
South Africa

Telephone:
0027 15 5563406

Website:
www.shiluvari.com

E-mail:
info@shiluvari.com

Sosian Lodge

S osian Ranch lies about fifty miles west of Mt Kenya in the wild Laikipia area. It offers pure wilderness, hundreds of birds, wild animals and beautiful landscapes. Guests are accommodated in a luxurious 1940s farmhouse, situated in a tropical garden overlooking Mt Kenya and miles of unspoilt Africa.

The lodge sleeps fourteen people with more space for children if needed and has a swimming pool, tennis court, and organic vegetable garden which provides ample supplies for the delicious cooking. Those with an adventurous spirit can really express themselves here by taking part in the many activities. One of the best ways to experience the African bush is on a horse, and Sosian provides horses for all levels of rider (though previous riding experience is required). There are also camels for riding; a different experience.

You can explore the bush on foot too. Led by a knowledgeable guide you'll learn about tracks and watch superb bird life. Game-drives take you further and closer to the game. Night drives are a speciality here, and seeking some nocturnal species after dark is an exciting way to see the bush. The really adventurous can head to the waterfalls on the Ewaso Narok River and jump thirty feet into a pool; or maybe just relax, and enjoy a picnic on the riverbank as colourful birds sing and the sound of rushing water encourages an afternoon nap.

INTRODUCTION

Rooms:
7 rooms (14 bed

Ave. Rates:
Approx $450
per adult
(all inclusive

Facilities:
Swimming po
tennis court, b
billiard room
electricity.

Activities:
Game drive
horse and car
riding, walkir
fishing, arche
bush meals
sundowne

58

S osian Lodge was a ruined farmhouse until 2000, when it was beautifully restored to accommodate guests on a stunning part of Kenya's Laikipia plateau. The Lodge supports the ranch, now a wildlife conservancy with the huge diversity of local animal and plant species, as well as creating jobs for local people.

Cattle ranching is another means of creating employment and the livestock and wildlife on Sosian co-exist extremely well, demonstrating how land can be used in several different ways to protect indigenous species while creating local wealth. All water used in the lodge is recycled and disposed of in the garden; any vegetable waste which is not fed to the domestic animals is composted and used in the vegetable garden.

Rainwater is collected from the roof and stored in tanks for drinking. The firewood that heats water for showers and is burned on open fires in the lodge in the evenings is dead wood collected from the ranch using a donkey cart. Any food not grown here is carefully selected to reduce packaging and purchased locally wherever possible to support rural communities. Local crafts are displayed in the lodge shop. All but five of the 100 staff are from the local area and have been trained on site. Guests are encouraged to explore Sosian with a guide, on foot, by camel or on horseback, and the road network is sparse to reduce impact on the landscape.

Sosian Lodge has been awarded the Eco Hotels of the World rating of 3 stars.

Address:
PO Box 6,
Rumuruti,
Kenya.

Telephone:
+254 (0) 62 31081

Website:
www.sosian.com

E-mail:
bookings@offbeatsafaris.com

Woodall Country House and Spa

Sundowner Deck

W oodall Country House and Spa is set amongst peaceful citrus orchards close to the Addo Elephant Park, only 45 minutes from Port Elizabeth in the malaria-free Eastern Cape. This boutique hotel is the ideal base from which to explore the adjacent Elephant Park, and nearby game reserves such as Schotia, Amakhala, Pumba, Kwantu and Elephant Back Safaris.

Each room is individually designed and boasts swirling ceiling fans, air conditioning, mosquito nets, heating, private verandahs, and en-suite bathrooms with separate bath and shower. All have private outdoor showers for an enlivening experience not to be missed. Stylish, regional cuisine is served in the thatched dining room with views of resident herons, cormorants and rare waterbirds. The cuisine is inspired by the flavours of local ingredients and freshly picked herbs and vegetables from the hotel's garden. Complementing the menu is the private cellar, boasting a unique and comprehensive selection of fine South African wines. The Spa, a sanctuary for relaxation, personal rejuvenation and serious pampering flows onto a salt-water pool, fringed with palms and a waterfall.

Facilities include a vitality studio, steam room, sauna, hydrotherapy bath and spacious double showers. The gym, a vibrant energetic space offers modern cardiovascular and strength training facilities. The adventurous can even experience game at close quarters from Woodall's open Landcruiser.

Facilities
Include:

CD Library
Cigar Selection
DVD Library +
Home Theatre
Health SPA
Gym, Library
Laundry and Iron
Fine restauran
Salt water poo
Tea/Coffee stati
Thatched sittin
room with firepl
Underground
wine cellar

★★★

Flora and fauna are an important part of Woodall Farm. Guests are encouraged to take part in environmental programs in the nearby Addo National park and the systematic planting of endemic plants has encouraged local wildlife to make it their home whilst also saving water.

Woodall's Safari Vehicle

Some clever energy saving techniques were incorporated into the original design of the lodge, where thatched roofs and an air-flow cooling system means that there is no need for air-conditioning in the dining room or lounge. Woodall Country House takes a keen interest in benefiting the community, and employs only local residents.

The staff support some worthwhile social schemes (like the Sunday River Valley HIV Aids Project) by donating used computers, magazines and equipment. Local wildlife is protected, thanks in part to the in-house ranger who can offer daily viewing tours to show and educate guests on the wonders that surround us here.

Luxury Room

Woodall Country House and Spa has been awarded the Eco Hotels of the World rating of 3 stars.

Address:
Woodall Farm
Jan Smuts Ave
Addo, 6105
South Africa

Telephone:
042 233 0128

Website:
www.woodall-addo.co.za

E-mail:
info@woodall-addo.co.za

Shopping Responsibly

This is a concept that can serve us well every day, not just when we travel. For many of us, shopping abroad and collecting souvenirs to remind, impress and amuse us is a quintessential part of the trip. As gifts they bring joy to the receivers, as activities they bring fun to the buyer and as products they bring wealth to far-flung corners of the earth.

On paper, shopping on holiday cannot possibly have any negative effect, but it does. We have all seen counterfeit souvenirs being sold to city tourists, and hurting big brands and stores. But it is in the wilderness that foreign money sometimes has its most disastrous consequences.

Every year customs officials make discoveries that border on the preposterous when they stop and search returning holidaymakers. Some people are still unaware of the devastating impact they have when they buy souvenirs made with parts of endangered animals or even living things. Amongst the most common finds are corals, reptiles, molluscs and orchids, and products made made from hunted tigers, rhinos, turtles and elephants. This is completely unacceptable; anyone who buys wildlife souvenirs, or souvenirs made from animal parts, endangers the natural world (the one they went to see).

Shopping abroad can be full of exciting new colours, sounds and smells and provide plenty of reminders of your time abroad without any need to damage the place. Try and find things that have been made locally by expert artisans, people who take pride in their work, If what you buy really is local, it will help direct your spending towards people who benefit the most. Haggling is fun and part of market life; approach it as such – it's not a battle to the death or a test of machismo, so be reasonable. A small amount of money for you might be a lot for the seller.

I know that in some areas begging will be widespread but – stay strong. If you want to help there are international organisations that you can contact to lend support. Money given to street beggars more often than not will go to a begging-gang leader. In really poor areas, I have found that little gifts (like cheap pens and notebooks bought at home) can help child beggars and are hard for a gang leader to use for anything else.

Your shopping at home may affect people abroad. At home, try to support shops that are environmentally and socially sound, that are ethical in their business dealings and will make sure that suppliers get fair prices for their product. Fair Trade products are easy to find and stores that make a firm statement of ethical principles can give a lot back and help make your money go further.

Useful Contacts:

WWF
www.wwf.org.uk
The WWF Souvenir Alert Campaign warns tourists against
buying souvenirs derived from endangered species.
A list of banned items can be found on their site.

Ethical Superstore
www.ethicalsuperstore.com
Offers eco-friendly shopping products such as ethical
gifts, green gadgets, fair trade and organic groceries.

Natural Collection
www.naturalcollection.com
Natural Collection is the UKs award-winning green sh
offering ethical, organic, fair trade, eco friendly produ

Get Ethical
www.getethical.com
A big selection of ethical, Fair Trade and environment
friendly products and services in one online shop.

Asia & Oceania

63

Bushy Point Fernbirds

B ushy Point Fernbirds Homestay B&B (Bed & Breakfast) is located on an eco-friendly, privately owned, managed and protected forest and wetland reserve on the edge of the New River Estuary, Invercargill, Southland. The property is included in the Awarua Ramsar Wetland; the word 'Ramsar' means it is of international importance. The owners have been restoration planting since 1992 and have made their project totally carbon neutral with zero impact on the wetland.

Predator mammals are under constant control on the reserve, and this has increased bird populations significantly. Fernbirds can often be seen very close to the boardwalk and heard calling from the house on a still evening. There are reports of reliable views for 99% of watchers. Good numbers of tui and bellbird provide a dawn chorus from the two guest rooms and can be seen feeding a metre away from the breakfast table. Amongst the most incredible sights are an Australasian Harrier roost nearby that draws a number of hawks back every night. Bushy Point Fernbirds is only a ten-minute drive from Invercargill, five minutes from the airport, and 25 minutes to Bluff port, making it ideal for stopping over before or after Stewart Island, Catlins or Fiordland. Start your New Zealand holiday here and recover from jet-lag surrounded by nature.

Bushy Point Fern birds Homestay

Rooms: 2
Ave. Price:
NZ$100 single
NZ$120 coup
breakfast inc.

Facilities:
Laundry,
Internet acce
TV lounge,
Kitchen.

★ ★ ★ ★ ★

Bushy Point Fernbirds B&B's incredible location allows a full natural immersion that you wouldn't expect in such conveniently placed accommodation. A number of energy saving ideas have been put into place here including efficient lighting and a heating system that runs on local firewood.

Deck Bedroom

Rainwater is collected from the roof and all cleaning products and water disposal allow for safe re-use of grey water in the gardens. Recycling is promoted on site for staff and clients alike and, as a result, waste is practically down to zero.

It is worth mentioning that Bushy Point Fernbirds was initially conceived as an experiment in eco activity to promote the maintenance of the forest and its bird population. Hospitality was a secondary activity but has proven successful and worthwhile. Guests can enjoy a very personal stay that can include guided walks around the beautiful, legally protected reserve.

Wetland Walk

Bushy Point Fernbirds has been awarded the highest "Eco Hotels of the World" rating of 5 stars.

Address:
197 Grant Rd
Otatara No 9RD
Invercargill
New Zealand

Telephone:
0064 032 131302

Website:
www.fernbirds.co.nz

E-mail:
inquiries@fernbirds.co.nz

Cloudlands

On the escarpment, nestled in the grounds of historic Cloudlands, in the Blue Mountains, is an old restored Writer's Retreat, offering elegant and spacious self-contained accommodation for two to seven people.

Ideal for couples, groups or executive retreats (there are four bedrooms: two doubles with queen-size beds, a twin and a single) this atmospheric, romantic lodge has beautiful timber features throughout and is set in over an acre of old terraced escarpment garden, which leads down to Prince Henry cliff walk.

Entrance

Rooms:
4 bedrooms

Private access t
scenic bushwalk
Walk to gallerie
restaurants and
the famous Thre
Sisters. Catch th
trolley bus to g
further afield. Ea
access to both
Katoomba and Le
shopping villages.
to the Vihara Bud
Centre, just dow
road from Cloudl
for morning/eve
meditations.

C loudlands is an historic property built with great care for the environment. The materials used as well as the site have created an energy-efficient property, warm in winter and cool in summer without any need for air-conditioning.

The gardens are fairly self-sustaining and guests are even able to select vegetables and herbs for their own cooking.

The Lounge

The property also keeps an eye on recycling and an advanced Bokashi internal composting unit is being fitted.

Guests are given demonstrations on the eco-quality of the property. These include an advanced water temperature system (a great energy-saver) and shower timers. There is also an interesting heritage walk that shows off the surrounding area and stresses that motor travel is usually unnecessary here. Local organic suppliers are used for food and packaging of all supplies. There is ample information available on local businesses as well as the many projects Cloudlands is involved in.

Cloudlands has been awarded the highest Eco Hotels of the World rating of 5 stars.

 Address:
4-6 Banksia,
Park Road Katoomba,
NSW 2780,
Blue Mountains,
Australia.

 Telephone:
+61 247827376

 Website:
www.cloudlands.com.au

 E-mail:
cloudlands@hermes.net.au

Main Bedroom

Cow Bay Homestay

Cow Bay Homestay is a Bed & Breakfast accommodation two hours' drive north of Cairns in the heart of the Daintree Rainforest, which is a World Heritage site. It is half-way between the Daintree River and Cape Tribulation, off the main tourist route, with easy access to many activities in the Cape Tribulation area, and the Daintree National Park.

At Cow Bay you can have a perfectly peaceful stay in a remote corner of North Queensland while getting an insight into an ecologically innovative, more sustainable lifestyle. Guests have beautiful views across the Alexandra Range and the hills of the National Park, where they are free to explore some of the untouched natural beauty Australia has to offer. Cow Bay beach is a fifteen-minute walk away and provides a beautiful remote spot for swimming, relaxing or basking in the sun.

Rooms:
1 Double Room
1 Queen Room

Ave. Rates:
overnight rate
minimum 2
nights $140.00
including
breakfast, $20 for
extra person or
child over 6 ye

Activities:
Bush walking
Swimming in
fresh water cre
Bird watching
Butterfly Watch
Wild life spotti
Star gazing,
Reading,
Relaxing

Cow Bay Homestay is entirely run on solar power. Energy is stored in batteries and a backup generator ensures no power failures. All new guests are briefed on the B&B's lights policy which is there to guard against energy wastage. The Homestay has its own borehole, providing water which is used throughout the house, and careful use of water is also explained to guests when they arrive.

The gardens are mulched to ensure their health and reduce water evaporation. Thanks to this they don't have to be watered regularly, but only rarely during the dry season. All detergents used are environmentally friendly so that harmful chemicals are not introduced into the waste water system.

Waste is sorted with care, and recycling is an important part of the business. Hosts ensure that organic material is composted. Cartons, glass and plastic are separated and guests are encouraged to separate their waste in the same way. Used or recycled items of value are donated to local charities. Given the importance of the local environment, the Daintree business community has always been striving for sustainability.

All local businesses support local produce and local tours. The Homestay helps by supplying a selection of herbs and products to restaurants and cafés. Its location on the edge of the National Park makes the hosts feel like custodians of the area; their work keeps this beautiful natural spot safe for the future. Cow Bay Homestay has been awarded the Eco Hotels of the World rating of 4 stars.

Address:
160 Wattle Close
Cow Bay
Qld 4873
Australia

Telephone:
(07) 4098 9151

Website:
www.cowbayhomestay.com

E-mail:
marion@cowbayhomestay.com

Eco Lodge Bali

A haven for nature lovers, Mountain Eco Lodge is located 750 metres up the slopes of Mt Batukaru in central Bali, only one and a half hours from Kuta and Ubud and two hours from the airport. The Eco Lodge enjoys spectacular views of southern Bali and the mountain peak, with protected rainforest only five minutes away. Each hand-crafted bungalow is surrounded by a lush tropical food-forest of cacao, coffee, coconuts, vanilla and jungle fruits.

You can enjoy a delicious healthy meal from the organic gardens either in the open-air restaurant or in your room. There are lots of great activities including informative rain-forest treks and food-forest walks, swimming in natural water-holes, walking in the Lodge's extensive gardens or just relaxing; and community workshops in Balinese massage, dance and costume, carving, making ceremonial offerings, and learning about plants used in Balinese medicinal healing.

Local Hindu ceremonies take place throughout the year and guests are welcome to join in. At Eco Lodge Bali you can expect personal and considerate service from the local staff who accept a maximum of ten guests and offer simply nature, relaxation and traditional Balinese culture.

Rooms:
4 Bungalows.

Ave. Rates:
US$99 - US$135

Facilities/Activities
Open air restaurant
Tea house, Rice
paddy & tropical
farmland walking
Guided mountain
trekking, Motorbike
tours, Car trips,
Transfers, Workshops
(20 different options
Massage, Traditional
Body treatment
Fish ponds, Natural
swimming holes
Monkeys, Internet
Vegetarian meals
available, Join
traditional ceremony

★★★★★

Eco Lodge Bali won the Wild Asia Responsible Tourism Award in 2007 as the best eco lodge in South East Asia. The Lodge limits its power usage and has been fitted with energy-efficient appliances including a solar-powered garden lighting system.

All grey water is re-used in nutrient beds and water saving showers are fitted. Staff hold weekly meetings to discuss sustainable management practices; the Lodge is involved in initiatives to minimise soil erosion caused by heavy rains, and is concerned with protecting over 800 hectares of native rainforest.

Eco Lodge Bali has been awarded the highest Eco Hotels of the World rating of 5 stars.

 Address:
Desa Sarinbuana Wanagiri
MT Batukaru Tabanan
Bali, Indonesia.

 Telephone:
+62 361 7435198

 Website:
www.baliecolodge.com

 E-mail:
ecolodgebali@yahoo.com

Esk Valley Lodge
from the Lawn

Esk Valley Lodge and Vineyard

Jes and Eileen Roddy will welcome you to their guesthouse, a fully restored building on the site of one of the earliest farms in the Esk Valley. Peace and privacy are a key feature yet the farm is only fifteen minutes from the restaurants of Ahuriri, the old fishing port of Napier. Its location makes it an ideal base from which to explore and enjoy northern Hawkes Bay, the local vineyards, Art Deco Napier, and the wild rivers, tranquil lakes and surf beaches of the area.

Esk Valley Lodge offers a comfortable, relaxing stay with excellent service standards which have earned it the Qualmark 4-Star Plus rating. The rooms are tastefully decorated, with high-quality bedlinen and furnishings. Each room has heat pumps for environmentally friendly heating and cooling. There is free wi-fi in all rooms and free use of the computer in the guest lounge. The full à la carte breakfast, which is included, features home-grown or local ingredients.

Rooms: 3.
All with separate
bathroom or ensuit

Ave. Prices:
High Season
NZ$ 160 - 220
(80 - 110 Euros)
Low season
NZ$ 150 - 195
(72 - 94 Euro)

Facilities
Orchard and garde
for guest use
Lawn sports - e.g
Petanque, croque
Free bicycles and
sports equipment
(e.g fishing rods)

E sk Valley Lodge is an excellent base for exploring the wonders of the valley, and once inside, its comfort and service can take your mind off the excellent work done on site to remain as eco-friendly as possible. Energy-efficient appliances and lighting have been fitted throughout and the Lodge boasts a centameter which monitors and logs electricity consumption to keep it low.

The staff have implemented alternative heating sources including local wood. There is no mains water so they are particularly keen on clever water management. Rainwater is collected and grey water is used in the garden. There is a modern septic tank system for waste and all bathrooms are fitted with low-flush toilets and low-pressure showers.

Here in the fertile Esk Valley staff can grow their own excellent produce by organic methods including, of course, compost heaps. The property has its own environmental statement, and all suppliers are selected for environmental awareness and minimal packaging. The vineyard is now seeking sustainable winegrowing accreditation. Esk Valley Lodge is an enthusiastic member of the NZ Organic Explorer eco-tourism listings and NZ Changemakers, which promote active citizenship.

Esk Valley Lodge and Vineyard has been awarded the Eco Hotels of the World rating of 3 stars.

The bedroom of the Sauvignon suite

View of Esk Valley and the Lodge looking west over vineyards

Summer wedding party in grounds of lodge

Address:
342 Hill Rd
Eskdale RD2
Napier
4182
New Zealand

Telephone:
64 6 8367904

Website:
www.eskvalleylodge.co.nz

E-mail:
info@eskvalleylodge.co.nz

Gecko Villa

G ecko Villa nestles amongst the paddyfields of Thailand's Isaan plateau. This private, three-bedroom getaway can be rented exclusively and is fully catered and serviced by expert staff. It enjoys a privileged position amid twenty hectares of gardens, orchards, woodlands, pastures and rice paddies.

Northeastern Thailand is the Kingdom's poorest area, yet it is famous for friendly and good-natured people who welcome those who make the effort to discover their home. Here, in the rural heartlands of Thailand still easily accessible by road, rail or air, you can relax among emerald paddy fields, and savour the forgotten rhythms of country life.

Gecko Villa presents a unique opportunity to immerse yourself in this unspoiled, largely undiscovered region of Thailand, to choose tranquillity and complete privacy and make this unique accommodation your own. Staff are on hand to show you the area, cook Thai food for you and introduce you to a way of life often forgotten or unappreciated.

Rooms:
3 bedroom
standalone villa

Ave. Price:
GBP 80

List of facilities/
activities availab

Private swimming
Deck & lounger
3 bedrooms,
Living & dining ro
Garden,
DVD, Satellite T
Fully equipped kit
Air conditionin
Freshly prepared m
Maid, Driver & fr
airport transfe
Thai massage
Thai cooking less
Local excursio

★ ★ ★ ★

Gecko Villa has no mains water so the staff rightly put water preservation at the top of their agenda. The water used in the Villa is treated and filtered naturally and traditional earthenware pots are used for rainwater collection.

Biodegradable or recyclable packaging is encouraged (for instance, banana leaf wrappers instead of plastic bags) and waste is kept to a minimum through an extensive recycling project involving the local community.

Part of the proceeds from Gecko Villa are used to fund reforestation and forest protection. The surrounding community are closely involved in running the Villa, with all supplies sourced locally or grown organically on site, and local staff who spend their income within the locality.

Address:
126 Moo 13,
Baan Um Jaan,
A. Prajak Sinlapakom,
41110 Udon Thani
Thailand

Telephone:
+66-81-9180500

Website:
www.geckovilla.com

E-mail:
info@geckovilla.com

Isaan, the poorest region of Thailand, has to date been uncharted territory for most overseas visitors. As the kingdom's most populous region, it has historically been targeted only by politicians seeking votes from debt-ridden rice farmers. Tourists have been driven off to the glitzy enclaves of Phuket, or to spend their dollars in five star hotels in Bangkok.

Properties like Gecko Villa and Green Gecko, in the rice fields outside Udon Thani, signal a new trend in choices made by visitors to the country, and underline the importance to hoteliers of providing unique and memorable experiences that also benefit the local community.

Gina's Beachfront
- Akaiami Island

Gina's Garden Lodges and Akaiami Beach Lodge

Gina's Aitutaki offers two locations: Gina's Garden Lodges in the lush setting of Tautu Village on the main island of Aitutaki, and Gina's Beach Lodges on the uninhabited island of Akaiami in the stunning Aitutaki Lagoon.

Both locations are family-friendly. The Garden Lodges are on the main island, and about five minutes' walk from the Tautu landing, on the Eastern shores of Aitutaki lagoon. The second, beachside property is situated on one of the reef islands at Akaiami Island, five miles away across the lagoon. This is Gina's Akaiami Beach Lodge.

They offer an environment that is special to Eastern Polynesia, and realise the Pacific dreams which cannot be found in an average resort hotel. These two secluded properties are ideal for honeymooners, but will appeal to any visitor who appreciates genuine Polynesian friendliness and charm.

Gina's Garden Lodges:
Prices Per Night :
Single $NZ75 ,
Double/Twin $NZ120.
There are family and
group rates

Amenities include:
Swimming Pool
and Sun Deck
Well Equipped Kitchen
Tea and Coffee
Refrigerator
Laundry Facility
Fans in Lodges
Television

Akaiami Beach Lodge
Prices Per Night:
Single $NZ180 ,
Double/Twin $NZ300

Amenities include:
Sited on a beautiful
sandy swimming bea
Doorstep access to
swimming and snorkel
Fully equipped kitche
Tea and Coffee
One single and one
double kayak for gue
use. Unobtrusive
caretaker on site

★★★★

This area of the world is very close to our idea of paradise. The beaches are white, the sea is an intense light blue and everywhere you look is teeming with wildlife and beauty.

You can enjoy the dream right on your doorstep, and yet here more than anywhere you are reminded of the fragility of nature and our responsibility to preserve it.

Gina's Garden Lodges and Akaiami Beach Lodges have been constructed in perfect harmony with their surroundings. The staff are attentive and welcoming whilst their expertise in natural concerns ensures that your stay has a minimum impact on the surroundings.

Energy conservation is ensured by the staff through notices and a regular check on appliances, and rainwater is collected for use in the laundry. The Lodges are involved in a number of local conservation projects to ensure that this corner of the planet stays looking like paradise for as long as possible.

Pool and Sundeck - Gina's Garden Lodges

Gina's Akaiami Beach Lodge - Akaiami Island

 Address:
P.O.Box 10,
Tautu Village,
Aitutaki Island,
Cook Islands,
South Pacific.

 Telephone:
(682) 31-058

 Website:
www.ginasaitutakidesire.com

 E-mail:
queen@aitutaki.net.ck

Glasshouse Mountains Ecolodge

Glasshouse Eco-Lodge is situated just four hundred metres from the foot of Mt Tibrogargan, surrounded by two hectares of gardens and forest running into a rainforest creek. There are more than eighty exotic tropical fruit trees on the property, and a vegetable patch that supplies the Eco-Lodge kitchen.

The eight rooms are attached to a 110 year-old wooden church. The Family Suite has a queen-size bed and its own bathroom, plus a twin-bedded loft bedroom. There are three Orchard Rooms (queen-size beds) with their own shower and WC; they all open onto a timber deck overlooking the orchard. The Forest Rooms have queen-size beds and a double bunk, and their own shower and WC.

Just behind the wooden church, you find the self-catering kitchen area in a restored railway carriage with two platforms for outside dining. The kitchen is equipped with stainless steel sinks, a gas hot-plate area, a fridge and microwave, pots and pans, a sandwich maker and a rice steamer. Crockery, glassware and cutlery are provided. Adjoining this is a second railway carriage — a leisure room in which to unwind, read a book or catch up on what is happening in and around the Eco-lodge.

Rooms: 8

Ave. Rates:
From $ 60.00
to $ 45.00 $AUD.

Facilities:
Self catering
fully equipped
kitchen, Guest
lounge.
Small conference
venue, Own
tropical fruits
orchard and
small rain-forest
re-forestation are
Guests can
participate in th
bird spotting proj
rare butterfly
project or simpl
relax in of the
many quiet spo
on the property

★ ★ ★ ★

Glasshouse Eco-Lodge has done an excellent job of monitoring consumption and ensuring total efficiency at every level of its operations. Electricity use is closely controlled and the usage gneerally costs less than 80 cents per guest per night.

All grey water is re-used in the extensive gardens from which guests are able to pick their own fruit. Fresh water is monitored so that the entire lodge uses 120 litres per day — less than the average Brisbane family would consume.

Waste is carefully separated and recycled and organic material is used for composting. The Lodge is involved in lots of eco projects including tree-planting schemes, and participates in the Government's Envirofund program which promotes cultivation of endemic plants. Glasshouse Eco-lodge has been awarded the Eco Hotels of the World rating of 4 stars.

Address:
Queensland
Australia
4518

Telephone:
61 7 549 30008

Website:
www.glasshouseecolodge.com

E-mail:
info@glasshouseecolodge.com

Great Ocean Ecolodge

The Great Ocean Ecolodge is a magnificent, multi award-winning environmentally sustainable guest house in the grounds of the Cape Otway Centre for Conservation Ecology. Adjoining the Great Otway National Park and close to the Great Ocean Walk, the Ecolodge is certified as an Advanced Ecotourism destination. The property has only five bedrooms, so every visit is unique and personal, particularly if you choose to book it exclusively. Bedrooms are private and peaceful, furnished with a comfortable bed, crisp clean linen, and timeless antiques. The en-suite bathrooms have fluffy towels and an assortment of locally made natural soaps and shampoos.

Wild kangaroos often gather nearby to graze in the early mornings and evenings. Watching the young bucks play-fighting and the does tending their joeys is a very special experience.

'Ecology Experiences' exclusive to Great Ocean Ecolodge guests offer outstanding opportunities for observing kangaroos, koalas and indigenous wild animals up close in their natural habitat. The Nature Studies Room and the Library are wonderful resources for checking on sightings and catching up on the finer points of natural history. At the end of every day you can round off your experiences with a meal in the Great Hall, where Ecolodge chefs serve tremendous feasts using only the freshest regional produce, much of it from their own garden.

Rooms: 5

Average price: $340 per double room per night includes afternoon tea, guided dusk walk to observe wildlife a continental breakfa ($40 from each room/night donate directly to conservation proje

Facilities: Restaurant, natur studies room, libra small conference facilities, free wirele internet, vehicle transfers to Grea Ocean Walk and i Great Otway Natic Park, wildlife rehabilitation cen bushland paths a grounds, wildlif observation equipn tours and conserva activities.

★ ★ ★ ★ ★

The Great Ocean Ecolodge runs entirely on solar power generated by a modern photovoltaic system and collects all its own water from the pristine rainfall of the Otways. The gardens consist entirely of indigenous plants, and an aerobic system ensures that waste water is used to maintain them. Food scraps are composted to fertilise the vegetable gardens or fed to the chickens who provide guests with fresh eggs daily. Supplies are selected from local sources to reduce food miles and the staff ensure they are not over-packaged to minimise waste.

Guest Bedroom

Education plays an important role at the Ecolodge and sustainability tours are available to introduce guests to the environmental aspects of the site. The Ecolodge is integrated within a Conservation Ecology Centre providing outstanding opportunities for guests to participate in a number of eco-activities and important local projects. Some of these have helped collect valuable knowledge on local flora and fauna that in turn continues to ensure its protection.

Orphaned koala joeys rehabilitating at the Centre

Great Ocean Ecolodge also operates a 24 hour Wildlife Rescue and Rehabilitation Centre, caring for injured and orphaned wildlife in the region. The Great Ocean Ecolodge has been awarded the highest Eco Hotels of the World rating of 5 stars.

Address:
635 Lighthouse Road
Cape Otway
Victoria
Australia

Telephone:
+61 352379297

Website:
greatoceanecolodge.com.au
www.capeotwaycentre.com.au

E-mail:
greatoceanecolodge@capeotwaycentre.com.au

Young kangaroo bucks play fighting

Green Gecko

The traditional "Sala" and pool at Green Gecko

Set in extensive grounds, with a private swimming pool, this traditional rural retreat is a great place to relax. Set among flowering gardens and plantations of tropical trees, sugar cane and cassava, it enjoys great views over the surrounding rice paddies. The villa's architecture is traditionally Thai: an impressive wooden staircase leads up to a raised and enclosed wooden deck with a delightful private swimming pool overlooking peaceful unspoiled countryside and evening sunsets.

Steeply pitched roofs with terracotta tiles lend the house an almost temple-like appearance. A raised sala here offers protection from the strong midday sun and views over the pool. Green Gecko has two eclectic and unique bedrooms, each of which is air-conditioned. The master bedroom is decorated with Thai motifs; it has a teak four-poster king-size bed with a soft cotton duvet and feather pillows, a large adjoining bathroom and WC, and an outdoor garden rain shower. The second bedroom features a queen-size four poster, again with a spacious adjoining bathroom / WC.

Green Gecko is located in Thailand's northeast region, the Isaan, about the minutes from Udon Thani airport. Frequent services arrive daily from Bangkok and Chiang Mai.

Rooms: 2,
with a large double be
airconditioning and
en-suite bathroom

Facilities:
Bed linen and
towels provided
Large living and
dining room
Satellite TV, Ipod do
DVD, Stereo and inte
Fully equipped Tha
and Western kitche
Large wooden deck
traditional "sala"
Private swimming p
with loungers
Extensive private gro
Covered car parki
Free airport transf

Local assistance
guides and drive
available, with veh
Thai cooking lesse

★★★★

Green Gecko is located in an area where natural resources are of utmost importance and where a balanced approach is paramount to ensure a happy coexistence with nature. Energy usage at the villa is efficiently controlled by eco-mode systems. There is no direct mains water so water is stored and collected with extreme care.

Biodegradable and recyclable packaging are used and local villages benefit from the re-use

The bedroom enjoys pool and woodland views

of some of these materials. Green Gecko was established to provide a direct source of sustainable income in one of the poorest regions of Thailand so social matters are at the top of the agenda. There is keen awareness of the need to protect local fauna and flora, instilled in childhood into people who have traditionally lived off the land. Green Gecko's design incorporates local features (construction on stilts, steeply pitched roofs, terracotta roof tiles) to maximise cooling and facilitate rainwater collection.

Part of the proceeds of Green Gecko go towards reforestation and protecting existing woodland from felling. Green Gecko has been awarded the Eco Hotels of the World rating of 4 stars.

A traditional buffalo cart still in use at Green Gecko

Address:
126 moo 13,
Baan Um Jaan
A. Prajak
Udon Thani 41110
Thailand

Telephone:
66-81-918 0500

Website:
http://www.thaivillarent.com

E-mail:
greengecko@thaivillarent.com

Jemby-Rinjah Eco Lodge

This is a unique eco-tourism escape in the heart of Australia's Blue Mountains. Here you can treat yourself to time away from the stress of modern life and relax in the calm of the mountains — only an enjoyable two-hour drive from the lights and noise of Sydney.

On arrival you will be struck by peace and quiet interrupted only by birdsong. Every morning parrots come to feed from your hand and lizards, possums, owls and nocturnal animals can be seen all around. Accommodation is in eco-friendly timber cabins and lodges, where the feather duvets and the slow-combustion wood fires are both comfortable and charmingly romantic.

You can enjoy a meal in the restaurant which serves delicious mountain cuisine. You can relax all day long on of the many verandahs around the main lodge or in the front porch where you can best soak-in the ambience. The Blue Mountains' most scenic lookouts and bush-walks are just a short stroll away.

Deluxe cabin at night

Rooms: 79

Ave. Price:
Cabins from
$170 p.n.
Eco lodge
B&B from
$89 p.p.p.n.

Facilities:
Self-containe
cabins, grou
eco lodges
state of the a
conference
centre, fully
licensed
restaurant
communa
BBQ area.

J emby-Rinjah Eco Lodge was designed and built with energy saving in mind. All structures are made with lightweight super-insulated timber to give a quick thermal response during their intermittent use.

The buildings are north-oriented for solar benefit and are well insulated using fibreglass and reflective foil to prevent condensation when it's cold. These kind of eco design ideas also take into consideration the finished style of the property. The cladding, for instance, is not only waterproof and sourced from local plantations, but also aesthetically beautiful, with a rustic finish that sits well in the surrounding environment.

Jemby-Rinjah Lodge was built on an existing degraded site which had been cleared for logging to supply a dolly-peg factory in nearby Blackheath Township. Cabin sites were selected to fit these cleared areas and existing fire-trails were used for transporting materials. All remaining trees and native vegetation were retained and since completion of the Lodge there has been a remarkable natural regeneration around the property. This principle of not disturbing the soil has been carried through to everything else. Boardwalks have been constrcted to house essential services and to give the builders a non-disruptive way of carrying materials in. The Lodge conserves water by having composting toilets, and waste is recycled on site so that everyday running is as low-impact as construction was.

Jemby-Rinjah Eco Lodge has been awarded the Eco Hotels of the World rating of 4 stars.

Conference centre at night

Eco-friendly boardwalks linking our eco lodges

Sunken lounge by the open fire

Address:
336 Evans Lookout Road,
Blackheath,
NSW 2785,
Australia.

Telephone:
61 (2) 4787 7622

Website:
www.jembyrinjahlodge.com.au

E-mail:
info@jembyrinjahlodge.com.au

Kingfisher Ecolodge

Kingfisher Ecolodge is located in Champasak Province, the southernmost province of Laos. This area, where Laos, Thailand and Cambodia meet, is also known as the Emerald Triangle. It offers guests a comfortable, intimate experience in an exotic setting that includes the northern wetlands of Xe Pian NPA (Natural Protected Area).

The owners aim to meet the expectations of those travellers who are looking for a different kind of tourism; who want to relax,but also to experience the environment and enjoy natural sights like grazing buffalos and elephants. The lodges were designed by Vincent Fischer Zernin and built using traditional building materials and techniques blended with modern concepts and architecture. The front wall of each room is made of glass so that guests can admire the landscape and the surrounding nature and enjoy a great sense of space. The hot-water shower room, which is separated from the toilet area, has a view onto the colourfully inviting wetland. Bungalow lighting is supplied by an individual solar system; all rooms have a ceiling fan and electrical plugs.

Rooms:
6 "Comfort bungalows" and
4 "Eco rooms"
which are more basic rooms with shared toile
Ave. Price:
Comfort bungalov
70US$
(incl. breakfast and tax).
Eco rooms: 23US

Facilities:
Internet point,
international phone calls and laundry are available.

★★★★

At Kingfisher Eco Lodge much imaginative thought has gone into creating spaces which perfectly marry modern tastes and comforts to traditional materials and know-how. Solar power provides lights and hot water in the rooms, all non-crucial electrical appliances are turned off in the evening and staff ensure that no lights are left on in unattended areas.

Kingfisher Bungalow verandah

Farm animals on site take care of food scraps while metals, carton, plastic, glass and aluminium are all dutifully collected and recycled. Another great side of the ecolodge is the community project which it supports. 5% of the income generated by the sale of eco activities (trekking, elephant-watching and so on) is given to the local primary school. Almost all supplies are bought locally and of course the activities are organised through the local community.

Kingfisher Bungalow view

Kingfisher Ecolodge has been awarded the Eco Hotels of the World rating of 4 stars.

Address:
Ban Khiet Ngong,
Champasak province,
Laos

Telephone:
030 5345016

Website:
www.kingfisherecolodge.com

E-mail:
info@kingfisherecolodge.com

Kingfisher Restaurant

Kosrae Village

Kosrae Village
Cottage

Kosrae is a stunningly beautiful island in Micronesia, with a high mountainous interior covered in lush rainforest jungle, surrounded by a pristine hard coral reef. The reef is extremely healthy and rich in invertebrate and fish life. Diving is suitable for both beginners and advanced divers.

Award winning Kosrae Village is tiny and very private. The cottages are built of local materials in the traditional style - thatch, mangrove timbers and reed siding. All cottages are surrounded by tropical foliage and nestled under large trees within fifty feet of the ocean. Every cottage (known locally as a lohm) has a private bath as well as a refrigerator and coffee maker.

There are great cultural tours, excursions to the Lelu and Menka ruins, outrigger canoe or kayak trips through the largest and oldest mangroves in the Pacific, rainforest hiking and climbing as well as snorkelling and scuba diving. The onsite restaurant is one of the best in the region, featuring local and Pacific Rim cuisine as well as vegetarian and international dishes.

Rooms:
10 Cottages

Inum Lounge
and Restaurant

5 Star Dive
Centre

Handicap
Accessible

★★★★

Kosrae Village ecolodge is a place where all efforts have been made to make sure it lives seamlessly next to the beautiful mangrove channel it borders. All power is turned off when the equipment is not in use, and its buildings have been designed to minimise the need for air conditioning and rely on natural airflow. Water is plentiful thanks to the high annual rainfall, but the need to conserve weighs heavily on the mind and Kosrae Village assiduously avoids the use of chemicals and ensures that other waste is kept to a minimum thanks to a comprehensive program of recycling.

Community work encourages and nurtures other eco-friendly activities, and staff are also involved in important conservation projects to monitor the coral and keep the beaches clean.

Kosrae Village has been awarded the Eco Hotels of the World rating of 4 stars.

Kosrae Village
Bungalow Interior

Address:
Kosrae Village Ecolodge and Dive Resort
Sleeping Lady Divers
Box 399
Kosrae,
Micronesia 96944

Telephone:
+ 691 370.3483

Website:
www.kosraevillage.com

E-mail:
info@kosraevillage.com

Kosrae Village
Bungalow Exterior

 Eco Lives

Kosrae Village and The Reef

There's an abundance of healthy marine life, hundreds of species of invertebrates and brilliant tropical fish. Barracuda, sharks, rays, dolphins and turtles thrive. This plus over 200 species of pristine hard and soft coral make it clear why this essential resource is one of Kosrae's most precious gems.

The 43 miles of breathtaking coral is protected by over fifty mooring buoys; it's among the most extensive buoy systems in the world.

Red Capital Ranch

Imagine a Manchurian hunting lodge nestled beside the Great Wall of China. Welcome to Red Capital Ranch by the Wall, Beijing's first and only eco-tourism resort, set on fifty-acre private estate with a 360° vista of the Great Wall of China from every one of ten ancient, restored, luxury Chinese villas.

Part of the Great Wall, dating to the First Emperor Qin Shi Huangdi, is on the estate in the former hunting lodge. This is now a fine restaurant offering sophisticated Manchurian cuisine, and you can also dine outside.

The Tibetan Tiger Lounge has views of the Great Wall and a beautiful stone fireplace where logs crackle in cool weather. At the Tibetan Secret Spa an array of soothing massage treatments greets wall-walkers seeking to relax after a day of adventure. The Great Wall of China can be reached from Red Capital Ranch within a matter of minutes, as the estate guards one of the ancient protected entrances. Ranch staff are always happy to prepare picnic lunches and lend backpacks on request.

Rooms:
8 double sui
2 XL dbl suit

Activities:
Yoga Area
Restaurant
Bar and Sp

Direct acce
to Great W

★
ECO - RATING

Red Capital Ranch is implementing a number of ecologically driven guidelines to maintain its eco-friendliness. Basic rules dictate that lights are not used in unoccupied rooms and there is a staff awareness campaign about water and power usage.

Some recycling is carried out and products bought from local producers or supplied by the organic garden. Staff are all local people.

Red Capital Ranch has been awarded the Eco Hotels of the World rating of 1 star.

Address:
No. 28 Xiaguandi Village, Yanxi Township, Huairou District,
Beijing 101407,
China.

Telephone:
+86 10 6402 7150/ 8403 5308

Website:
www. redcapitalclub.com.cn

E-mail:
info@redcapitalclub.com.cn

Sukau Rainforest Lodge

S ince the opening of this 20-room ecolodge in 1995 there has been a continuous effort to improve its facilities and to fine-tune the natural experience on offer. In 2001 a major project was the new Melapi Restaurant and jetty complete with fishing and sunset decks. In 2002 four bird- and wildlife-viewing decks were added, as well as a 1,500 ft long covered Hornbill Boardwalk, complete with two elephant passes to accommodate their regular migration through the back of the lodge.

All twenty rooms are equipped with twin beds, ceiling fan, mosquito net, dressing table and fully tiled en-suite bathroom and WC with hot water, shampoo and soap dispensers. Nearby activities include river cruises, jungle walks, night cruises, bird watching, abseiling, fishing and wilderness camping. Many projects have been carried out here over the years under the banner of Sukau Ecotourism Research and Development Centre (SERDC), including weed clearing, water-tank building, wildlife rehabilitation, tree planting, medical research and more. The Lodge sets aside US$1 nightly for every international adult guest as a contribution to community and environmental projects.

INTRODUCTION

Rooms: 20

Average Rates:
Packages only
contact for deta

Activities:
River cruises to
view exotic
wildlife, Jungle
boardwalks,
Night cruise
(chargeable)

★★★★

The Sukau Rainforest Lodge is situated in an area where conservation is a primary concern and where every small part of the visitor's footprint makes a big impression on the environment. As a result, the staff are well trained in all sorts of clever environmental techniques and guest education is key to running the property.

Although surrounded by water, the lodge has to make use of filtration systems to make sure that river water can be safely used in the bathrooms and rainwater can be used for cooking and, of course, drinking.

One of the unique features of this lodge is its proximity to elephants. The staff use collected elephant dung to fertilise a tree planting project, which is forming a significant wildlife corridor nearby. During one of their outings guests discover that the Lodge considers conservation on their small launches, which run on tiny smokeless motors. Even the life jackets are black, so as not to disturb the local wildlife.

Suhau Rainforest Lodge has been awarded the Eco Hotels of the World rating of 4 stars.

Address:
Lot 1, Pusat Perindustrian
Kolombong Jaya,
Mile 5.5, Jalan Kolombong,
88450 Kota Kinabalu,
Sabah, Malaysia

Telephone:
+60 898 45100

Website:
www.sukau.com

E-mail:
info@sukau.com

The Orchid

Built according to strict ecological principles, The Orchid is surrounded by lush gardens and it's just a whisper away from the domestic airport. Despite the location, it's a serene place, and everything is modern and understated. There's a rooftop pool and restaurant with good views over the airport and city.

Although it looks like yet another grand airport hotel, The Orchid was built using sustainable materials and designed to require minimal heating, lighting and electricity. Which is not to say that you don't get every conceivable five star luxury for your money - rooms have been decorated with flair, and all have mood lighting and writing desks with built-in internet hubs.

The shared spaces are just as welcoming. It's a real pleasure to slip into reed slippers and cotton robe and kick back with a page-turner beside the rooftop pool. The Orchid is hidden in a leafy garden, contributing to the atmosphere of calm and seclusion. Befitting a luxury airport hotel, there's a 24-hour coffee shop, a bar and nightclub and an impressive selection of restaurants.

Rooms: 245

Business Use
Airport Close

Facilities:
Rooftop Poo
Fitness Centr
Laundry
Airport
transfers

★ ★ ★ ★ ★

The Orchid is an interesting proposition in that it's a luxury hotel in a convenient city location yet it has spent an incredible amount of effort and money on achieving the highest possible eco ratings.

Starting with the construction and design and the implementation of some of the very latest architectural and engineering techniques, the Orchid follows the three-R mantra to reduce, re-use and recycle. This is demonstrated in features from water treatment and conservation to energy saving and housekeeping practices.

The Orchid has been awarded the highest Eco Hotels of the World rating of 5 stars.

Address:
70-C, Nehru Road,
Adjacent to Domestic Airport,
Vile Parle (E),
Mumbai 400 099,
India.

Telephone:
022-26164040

Website:
www.orchidhotel.com

E-mail:
envohmu@orchidhotel.com

Enjoy the coolness of ozone treated water

Tree Tops Jungle Lodge

Elephant photo taken at the lodge in July, the dry season.

S taying at Tree Tops is an extraordinary adventure, completely immersed in nature. You'll bathe in a freshwater well, forget about electricity, and eat meals cooked on a wood fire. The unfenced lodge provides an awesome vantage point from which to watch jungle life. Wild animals come and go as they please and the atmosphere is charged with the noise and energy of the wild. The clay huts are simple and rustic, similar to traditional local huts.

They combine traditional building methods with fresh ideas on design, strength, and function. The tree huts are inspired by traditional chena tree huts from which the local farmers watch their cultivated plots safe from wild animals, especially elephants. Since 1997 the lodge has been a private nature retreat and a base for environmental activism. Preservation of the remaining forest and its wildlife have been the main priority. From 2002 it opened to tourists, still with the intention to preserve, but also to teach and reveal the wonders of nature. A jungle hide-out, it is situated in the middle of a main elephant track which in the past as part of a set of paths used by illegal hunters and loggers. The idea is to try and function as an obstacle for those people who seek the destruction of this beautiful environment, while at the same time helping to generate alternative means of income for local staff.

Rooms: 4
2 tree huts
2 mud houses

English speaking
local naturalists

Tracker team

Cooks

24 hours staff

Freshwater well

Charging facility
for cameras

Small library

★ ★ ★ ★ ★

There is no electricity at Tree Tops Jungle Lodge. This is not only for environmental reasons but is a purposeful effort to live in harmony with the wild elephants that move completely undisturbed around the lodge. Tree Tops has constructed two freshwater wells to support it through the dry season. This makes it self-sufficient; guests have enough for drinking and bathing without harming the environment.

Fresh water well situated 100 metres from the main lodge

Waste disposal is kept in check as the lodge is small and everything possible is re-used by their staff. They have personal reasons to be eco-aware. In 2002 they fought the local council to prevent this beautiful elephant grazing area from being used as a disposal ground, and built a roadblock to protect it. In Tree Tops was born from a desire to protect the land and inform people of the importance of a habitat so crucial to wild elephants. Helped by ethical tourism they hope to educate the world in their fight for preservation.

Tree Tops open plan area with large table for the meals

100% of the staff are recruited from the local community and trained by the owner. The philosophy is to do everything the local way and highlight the beauty of these ancient customs and practices. This is an important step into giving environmentally and socially acceptable employment to people who might otherwise be tempted by illegal logging or hunting.

Tree Tops Jungle Lodge has been awarded the highest Eco Hotels of the World rating of 5 stars.

Tree Tops Thatched Mud Hut

Address:
Weliara Road
Buttala
Sri Lanka

Telephone:
+94(0) 777 036 554
+94(0) 715 202 651

Website:
www.treetopsjunglelodge.com

E-mail:
treetopsjunglelodge@gmail.com

Ulpotha

Ulpotha has been a pilgrimage site for thousands of years and remains an oasis of tranquillity in the heart of Sri Lanka. It is a beautiful private hideaway, open to guests for part of the year; a place of total peace, where you can experience the warmth, generosity and gentle hospitality which Sri Lankans love to offer.

Ulpotha is a traditional working village cradled on the one side by low mountains and a lotus-ringed lake, and on the other by tiny, emerald green paddy fields. The focus, at present, is on restoring an ageless agricultural way of life, including bio-diverse organic farming and reforestation.

Guests are welcome to Ulpotha and those who come will find a natural sanctuary of exceptional beauty where the main activity is simply relaxing in its remarkable atmosphere of peace and calm. Yoga classes are held twice daily and traditional Ayurvedic treatments are available at the treatment centre.

INTRODUCTION

Rooms:
Max 19 guests
double + twin
huts and one
triple hut.

Activities:
Yoga classes,
massage,
Ayurveda,
steambath,
saunas,
swimming,
walking,
mountain
climbing.

★ ★ ★ ★ ★

Lighting at Ulpotha is provided by kerosene and coconut oil lamps. No electricity is used. Water is provided by a tanque (a man made lake) rehabilitated by Ulpotha that not only sustains the guests but is also used by over 200 local farmers further down the watershed. This project also spurred the planting of over 5,000 trees.

This is more than a place to stay. The villagers have been able to demonstrate their local expertise here and guests learn and contribute to the culture.

The most fundamental of Ulpotha's environmental policies is to limit the number of guests it accepts (no more than nineteen at once) and the hospitality period (at most 26 weeks a year). Ulpotha runs a free Ayurvedic clinic treating over 100 villagers per week. Guests visit and can participate in the clinic. Ulpotha has helped rebuild and maintain most of the communal institutions in the immediate area including the local school, hospital and temple.

Ulpotha has been awarded the highest Eco Hotels of the World rating of 5 stars.

Address:
Flat 36,
Galle Face Court 2
Colombo 03
Sri Lanka.

Telephone:
+44 208 123 3603

Website:
www.ulpotha.com

E-mail:
info@ulpotha.com

Local Food and Wine

In our busy modern lives it seems of little consequence where our food comes from. At times we don't even seem to mind what it tastes like! This is of course a sad result of our continuous drive to over-industrialise in the cause of buying cheap and selling dear. Fortunately, some good restaurants and increasingly demanding consumers are bringing about a food revolution that promises the return of old fashioned values, and local produce grown with pride, passion and even love.

On holiday we pay even more attention to food and drink. We're there to taste local specialities and we have time to enjoy them, often in good company. Our Eco hotels favour foot grown by local producers in a sustainable way, organically and with mimal impact on the environment. Organic and biodynamic products are more easily available as producers pursue quality and insist that the kitchens of every eco property should be full of the best ingredients. Fair Trade is a much-publicised initiative. Small producers are able to compete and make a living, which in turn allows them to be self-sufficient.

Choosing Fair Trade and organic food is not about fashion; it's the only choice if we want to sustain a healthier economy and promote better products. As a consumer there are things you can do at home and on holiday. Buy seasonal food to encourage local producers and cut the carbon emissions built up by food miles incurred in long-distance freight. If you choose to eat local specialties, artisans all over the world are helped and you ensure the survival of their specialities. Choosing unusual local foods also helps preserve the biodiversity of food products. In Europe alone, 75% of produce bio-diversity has been lost since 1900. All over the world, 30,00 vegetable varieties have become extinct. We are losing unusual flavours in exchange fo mass produced, cheaper food that will become tedious.

In every Eco Hotel we have listed, owners select supplies with care; in many you can enjoy fabulous organic meals offered by local chefs who know their ingredients and th producers well.

Useful Contacts:

The Fairtrade Foundation - www.fairtrade.org.uk
An independent certification body which awards the FAIRTRADE Mark to products which meet international Fairtrade standards, as a guarantee that disadvantaged producers are getting a better deal

Slow Food - www.slowfood.org.uk
Slow Food is an international eco-gastronomic movement which promotes the enjoyment and protectio of locally produced food products and regional cooking.

Central & South America

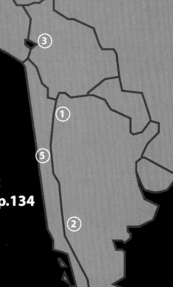

Argentina
1) Estancia and
   Bodega Colomé - **p.118**
2) Estancia Peuma
   Hue - **p.120**

Bolivia
Chalalan - **p.110**

Brasil
Eco-Lodge Itororó - **p.116**

Chile
Ecocamp Patagonia - **p.114**

Costa Rica
Arenas del Mar - **p.106**
Danta Corcovado Lodge - **p.112**
La Cusinga Lodge - **p.122**
Lapa Rios Ecolodge - **p.124**
The Pacuare Jungle Lodge - **p.132**
The Tirimbina Rainforest Center - **p.134**

Ecuador
Black Sheep Inn - **p.108**

Guadeloupe
Le Parc aux Orchidées - **p.126**

Nicaragua
Los Cardones - **p.128**

West Indies
Paradise Bay - **p.130**

Arenas del Mar

A renas del Mar is a beach and nature resort located next to Manuel Antonio National Park on the Pacific coast of Costa Rica. It offers a luxurious holiday in harmony with Costa Rica's natural beach and rainforest. Guest rooms, apartments and suites offer spectacular ocean views and fine dining in two hotel restaurants, with a focus on fresh local products and personalised service.

Arenas del Mar is the perfect base from which to explore the area around Manuel Antonio and Quepos on the Central Pacific coast of Costa Rica. You can enjoy white-water rafting, mangrove kayak and boat tours, guided rain-forest hikes, ocean kayaking, catch and release fishing, canopy tours of the forest, and horseback riding excursions.

The hotel aims to gain a Certificate for Sustainable Tourism from the Costa Rican Tourism Ministry, and this has guided its building and operation. Sustainability is a key at all levels.

Arenas del Mar Beach and Nature Resort has 38 guest rooms, including ocean view apartments with two bedrooms and three bathrooms. Other facilities include a small spa located below the main restaurant with breathtaking views of Manuel Antonio National Park and the Pacific Ocean, a gift shop featuring local art and souvenirs and a sophisticated business centre.

Rooms: 38

Ave. Rates:
From $200 in
Low Season to
$795 in
Holiday Season

Activities:
Manuel Antonio
National Park,
Canopy Tour,
Rainmaker Tour
Damas Island
Mangrove by Kayak
Butterfly & Aqua
Gardens Nature
Reserve, Morning
or Sunset Sailing
White Water Raft
Horseback Riding
Surf Lessons

★ ★ ★ ★ ★

A renas del Mar has only been in business for a few months yet its rigorous energy saving plan and aggressive carbon neutral project has earned widespread recognition.

The emphasis is on minimal impact and local fauna conservation. Power lines have been moved underground to protect monkeys and other wildlife. Solar panels supplement the hot-water supply. The property runs on energy-efficient equipment and lighting, with advanced air conditioning and refrigeration technology. Both management and staff have been rigorously trained in energy saving, and starting this year, an annual energy saving report will dictate goals for the following year.

Grey water is recycled. All cleaning and personal products offered to guests are biodegradable. Information about water saving techniques is available to guests and there is a linen and towel re-use program. Arenas del Mar recycles from all areas of the hotel, including the kitchens where composting facilities are installed, and makes every effort to educate guests on the importance of sustainability.

They can also meet local people and see how they live; guided tours visit local communities and conservation projects, and a planned sustainability tour will examine numerous projects and practices in sustainable tourism.

Arenas del Mar has been awarded the highest Eco Hotels of the World rating of 5 stars.

Address:
Manuel Antonio Hotel
Costa Rica

Telephone:
011-506-777-2777

Website:
www.arenasdelmar.com

E-mail:
info@arenasdelmar.com

Black Sheep Inn

Black Sheep Inn is an inexpensive, ecologically friendly hotel high in the Andes Mountains of Ecuador. Perched on a hillside, this rural eco-lodge is a perfect place to discover centuries-old culture and diverse ecosystems.

It offers comfortable affordable accommodation and a great base for day hiking, horseback riding, mountain biking, acclimatising and exploring indigenous markets. Black Sheep Inn is a Bed & Breakfast which features gourmet vegetarian food with organic produce from its own gardens, and is perfectly located for backpackers, eco-tourists, hikers, on a family holiday or just interested in wildlife and relaxation.

Black Sheep Inn in is also a serious pioneer in the world of eco tourism, having been shortlisted for some important awards and winning prestigious prizes, as well as being eco-certified by the Ecuadorian Ministry of Tourism.

The Inn is involved in interesting social projects, including the setting-up of a local library. Altogether it is an organic project that, over the years, has improved local life through ecological awareness and social well-being.

Rooms:
9 rooms max
capacity 30

Ave Rates:
US$25 to US$70
p.p. per night
includes dinne
and breakfast.

Facilities:
internet, full ba
sauna, hot tub
waterslide,
frisbee golf,
horseshoes,
volleyball,
treehouse,
zipline/cable sw
farm animals

★ ★ ★ ★ ★

Black Sheep Inn is one of those places where technical ingenuity has given guests all they want while maintaining the balance of nature. Electricity and water consumption are seriously monitored and considerable work has been carried out to ensure that equipment like light bulbs, computers and stoves are as efficient as possible.

There is a thermal siphon on the wood-heated sauna that also heats the hot tub (without electricity!) and the highest solar powered waterslide in the world. All waste water is processed. Toilets are the dry-compost kind and roof water is collected for irrigation. Recycling is rigorous and the Inn is proud to achieve zero waste. This efficiency has spread to the general community as the Inn has spearheaded construction of a Community Recycling Center.

The Black Sheep Inn is efficient both socially and ecologically. The staff have created a comprehensive and pioneering philosophy and it's kept them at the forefront of the eco-hospitality industry. Black Sheep Inn has been awarded the highest Eco Hotels of the World rating of 5 stars.

 Address:
PO Box 05-01-240
Chugchil.n
Cotopaxi
Ecuador.

 Telephone:
(593) 328 145 87

 Website:
www.blacksheepinn.com

 E-mail:
info@blacksheepinn.com

Chalalán

C halalán is the story of a dream come true; a dream that was born in the Bolivian Amazon, in the community of San José de Uchupiamonas: an ecolodge, designed to blend in with its environment using ancient building techniques and environmentally-friendly local materials.

Attention went into every detail so that any adventure would be as comfortable as possible. This is a place where you can relax and enjoy warm breezes, the sounds of nature and delicious home cooking.

Located in one of the richest protected areas of the planet, known by scientists as a Biodiversity Hotspot, this tropical paradise has the highest possible biodiversity of indigenous life. There are some 45,000 different plant species and over 1,000 tropical bird species whose songs will wake you up in the morning.

Chalalán was Highly Commended as 'Best In a Park or Protected Area' by the Virgin Holidays Responsible Tourism Awards of November 2007.

Rooms: 13
(10 in twin/triple/dou
(3 exclusive cabins
with private bath
Capacity: 30 gues

Average price:
Usd 330 per perso
for 3days/2night

List of facilities/
activities availabl

Transfer In/Out Airp
meals during your s
bilingual native gu
Madidi National P

Hiking, night hik
night canoe trip
camping, rainfor
interpretation,
medicinal plant
birdwaching,
wildlife wiewin
cultural tours
and much mor

★ ★ ★ ★ ★

Nestling inside the protected Madidi National Park, Chalalán was crafted with eco-tourist in mind, respecting its natural surroundings and using only local materials for construction. Power comes only from the sun and a sophisticated waste water treatment system has earned the lodge a highly acclaimed certification from the Bolivian Ministry of Sustainable Development.

Design and distribution of the ecolodge's rooms were planned down to minute detail with the advantage of jungle knowledge. The walls are made from the Copa Palm Iriartea Deltoidea, and covered with matting; the roofs are woven with asaí palm leaves Geonoma Deversa, and the floors are made of fine hardwood.

Chalalán has implemented an educational program to provide environmental information. This promotes preserving natural heritage and protecting indigenous communities. The ecolodge generates direct economic benefit for the local community during the tourist season by offering 37 employment opportunities within the lodge and sixty for local families.

Address:
La Paz: 189 Sagarnaga Street
(Shopping Dorian)
2nd Floor, Office # 22
Bolivia

Telephone:
(591) 223 114 51

Website:
www.chalalan.com

E-mail:
chalalan_eco@yahoo.com

Danta Corcovado Lodge (DCL)

Danta Corcovado Lodge is a 35 hectare farm located in Guadalupe, La Palma, only five miles from the Los Patos sector of the Corcovado National Park, and the closest place to the Guaymi Indigenous Reserve. The Lodge is a local family business and aspires to be a leader and an example of ecological design and creativity, conservation and sustainability in the beautiful Osa Península.

All wood used in the lodge's construction is made from reforested wood that the owner's father, Juvenal, planted 15 years ago. Details are uniquely designed from leftover stumps, branches, and odd pieces left behind by the neighbours; here at Danta nothing goes to waste. The rooms are a delightful combination of simplicity with a splash of whimsical creativity: polished teak floors, ceiling fans, screened twisted branch windows, comfortable Surá beds with unique towering headboards, tree 'cookie' mirrors and bedside tables, clean and colourful bedding and towels, and many more distinctive details.

Rooms:
Main Lodge: 4
No. of Bungalows

Ave. Rates:
Rooms - $60
Bungalows - $9

Facilities:
Parking, Private
Trails, Library,
Lounging areas
Laundry Service
Handicap-friend
facilities (one
room available
with private ba
& shower),
Typical Costa Ric
meals for gues
only (daily mer
No pets pleas

112

D anta Corcovado Lodge (DCL) was built to a rustic design that not only harmonises with nature but also ensures maximum energy efficiency by allowing for optimal use of sunlight during the day. More energy saving techniques such as light-saving bulbs, staff checks and a lights-off policy ensures that the nights are also environmentally sound.

The Lodge's location amid the lush tropical rain-forest of the Osa Peninsula means water is plentiful, but its ultimate treatment does affect preservation of the beautiful surroundings. Safeguards include a towel and linen re-use program and biodegradable products for all washing. Grey and black water is purified through a wetland system, the only one in the area.

Danta Corcovado Lodge runs a continuing education program to demonstrate the importance of recycling. Organic waste feeds farm animals and the organic garden is maintained by local women. This aspect of the lodge is interesting, as you find a sense of social commitment not only in applyng green policies but in getting local people equally involved.

The staff are active in community associations, and are part of Rainforest Alliance's pilot program for sustainable tourism with an internal Green Team. Their biggest project, UPE Guadalupe, is building a local community centre and health clinic. This will help several under-served rural communities, including the Guaymi Indigenous Reserve. UPE Guadalupe aims to be a sustainable community development that fosters micro businesses, cultural exchange, health and education.

Danta Corcovado Lodge has been awarded the highest Eco Hotels of the World rating of 5 stars.

 Address:
Apartado Postal 83-8203,
Puerto Jiménez,
Costa Rica

 Telephone:
(506) 735 1111

 Website:
www.dantacorcovado.net

 E-mail:
info@dantacorcovado.net

Ecocamp Patagonia

EcoCamp Patagonia offers a compromise between hotel accommodation and camping. When you arrive in Torres del Paine National Park you'll be delighted by its large dome-shaped tents – which offer simple but important luxuries like being able to stand up straight and lie down on a real bed. Nearby you have the rather more lavish luxury of an excellent dining tent, offering good local food. The discomforts of traditional camping don't exist here yet the excitement of close contact with nature is still very much the main attraction.

Tours (in English) include trekking, wildlife journeys and photography safaris. Whatever your interests, this is a great place to unwind and enjoy the wonders and beauty of Patagonia.

The basic premise of the EcoCamp was to maintain the nomadic spirit of the ancient inhabitants. In this area they moved along the coast looking for food and shelter, living in harmony with nature and building huts out of organic wood, fur and leather. Patagonia EcoCamp's design was inspired by these traditional Kawesqar huts.

Rooms:
15 Standard
Domes (32 gues
6 Suite Dome
(12 guests)

Ave. Rates:
The average
price for a 4-
day program
is USD 1,40(
per person
(DBL basis)

Activities:
Trekking, Hiki
Birdwatchin
Wildlife watch
Relaxing, Walk
Sightseein

★ ★ ★ ★ ★

EcoCamp has achieved the highly coveted ISO 14001 qualification. All energy used on site is produced from renewable sources like water, sunlight and wind. Summer days here can have seventeen hours of daylight, so solar panels operate extremely well, and are complemented by two wind generators. The site is also justifiably proud of its waste management system which includes state-of-the art composting toilets with solid/liquid waste separation. These are the first of their kind in Patagonia.

The Ecocamp guides undergo wilderness training that allows them to guide guests through the beautiful but demanding environment. Despite the remote location social interaction is important and the camp takes great pride in employing local staff including artists who are asked to decorate the tents and craftsmen who accessorise them.

The construction of the camp is in itself something of a natural wonder. Exacting criteria were met when placing the tents. All construction is upon raised platforms to allow free circulation of wild animals beneath, buildings are connected by walkways for the same reason and there are no fences around the EcoCamp so horses can come in and freely graze in the mornings. Solar lamps light all the walkways and domes at night. These are not only eco-fantastic but produce subtle tones that avoid disturbing night animals. EcoCamp Patagonia has been awarded the highest Eco Hotels of the World rating of 5 stars.

Address:
Don Carlos 3219,
Las Condes,
Santiago,
Chile

Telephone:
Toll Free USA + Canada: 1-800-901-6987
Toll Free UK: 0-800-051-7095

Website:
www.ecocamp.travel

E-mail:
info@ecocamp.travel

Eco-Lodge Itororó

Itororó means 'the whispering of the waters' in the language of the Tupi-Guarani. The reference is evident in the nearby brook, which provides the Inn with purest water always at the perfect temperature. The secluded location offers a great opportunity to relax as well as a range of activities from hiking tours to horseback riding and of course swimming in the crystal-clear natural pool.

Eco-Lodge Itororó offers simple and cosy accommodation in inviting log houses. Its philosophy is closely modelled on ideals formulated by Dr. Fritz Dungs when he came here to study and protect endemic orchids; it was here that he was based and from here that he set out on expeditions. The result was Orchidaceae Brasilienses, co-authored with G.F. Pabst and the seminal work on Brazilian orchids.

INTRODUCTION

Rooms:
10 Doubles
4 Singles

Facilities:

Natural
swimming poc
Waterfall
in the summe
Trekking and
Hiking
Orchid Garde
200.000 squar
meters of
Atlantic Rainfor

Nearby:
Paragliding,
Rafting,
Mountain biki
Horse riding

E co-Lodge Itororó has been blessed with a source of fresh clean water; the staff appreciate that and make sure that no chemicals are released into it. Energy is mostly solar and all outdoor lighting is turned off by 10pm. As the city is far away there is an effort to remain self-sufficient in waste disposal. All waste is separated and organic waste is composted and used in the grounds.

Restoration of the forest's environmental balance is Eco-Lodge Itororó's main goal, so the management have initiated projects to fight against non-native plantations which have been replacing indigenous plants and consequently have reduced local fauna to dangerous levels. Where pilot projects have removed non-native plants in favour of endemic species, the ecosystem is thriving.

The staff here take their projects extremely seriously and all new developments are carefully documented so that their efforts will benefit similarly endangered environments.

Eco-Lodge Itoró has been awarded the Eco Hotels of the World rating of 3 stars.

Address:
Rainer Dungs
Estrada do Curuzu s/n
C.P. 96.675
Nova Friburgo, 28.600-000
Brasil

Telephone:
0055-22-99074912

Website:
www.ecolodge-itororo.com

E-mail:
info@ecolodge-itororo.com

Estancia and Bodega Colomé

Colomé was farmed for thousands of years by native Indians who were excellent stewards of the land. As the tale goes, the Indian chief Colomin received vines from the Spanish conquistadores in the late sixteenth century for good services rendered.

The old Colomé winery was founded in 1831, probably by the last Spanish governor of Salta, Nicolás Severo de Isasmendi y Echalar. In 1854 his daughter, Ascensión, married José Benjamín Dávalos, and introduced pre-phylloxera Malbec and Cabernet Sauvignon vines to Colomé from France. Three vineyards dating from this time still produce grapes. Colomé is considered the oldest working winery in Argentina.

Finca Colomé has only 7 suites in total, each charmingly decorated and with striking views of the surrounding countryside. Accommodation is based on full board and includes use of all the estancia's facilities, including a meditation and yoga room, swimming pool, tennis court, and walking trails. You can indulge yourself in Finca Colomé with fabulous local wine and home-cooked food surrounded by some of the most incredible scenery in South America.

Rooms: 9

Ave. Rates:
On Request

Activities:
Horse riding
Trekking
Mountain biki

ECO - RATING

As a working winery, the Estancia has a deep understanding of local conditions. Water in Colomé is such a rarity that the very little available is treated as liquid gold. Here it is also a source of energy and almost 80% of the property's power comes from a water turbine.

All the vineyards and vegetable gardens are organic, which means that only natural compost is used. Separation of waste is taken seriously and the Estancia is actively involved in all aspects of recycling from plastics to organic. Estancia Colomé has been awarded the highest Eco Hotels of the World rating of 5 stars.

Address:
Ruta Provincial 53,
km 20 4419 Molinos,
Province of Salta,
Argentina.

Telephone:
0054 3868 49 4200

Website:
www.estanciacolome.com

E-mail:
info@estanciacolome.com

Estancia Peuma Hue

Peuma Hue means 'place of dreams' in the native Mapuche language and it is idyllic; the moment you see it you know you are somewhere special.

Peuma Hue originated in a project to preserve the local forest. A recycled log cabin provided a great starting point for the creation of a ranch, and the property now includes a mountain cabin, two log cabins, a barn, a carpentry workshop, a boat-house and a meeting room.

Work here continues to evolve organically and the staff take great pride in maintaining the land, garden, greenhouse and hiking trails. Guests can immerse themselves in a rich natural environment where numerous species of birds, Patagonian hares, wild boars and trout live happily in harmony with the lodge.

Rooms: 12

Facilities:

500 acres of
mountains, valley
forests and waterfa
all in the midst of
National Park
2 miles of lakefro
pebble beach
4 houses for gues
Meeting and
dining buildinç
Non-denominatic
Temple
Organic garde
and greenhous
Stables

W ith eight rooms and two log cabins the Estancia Peuma Hue nestles seamlessly in the middle of the National Park. The park administrators enforces environmental protection regulations, so along with the staff's know-how this creates an efficient and low-footprint place to stay.

The investment in green energy is not yet 100% yet but a complete switch to renewable sources is coming soon. Water is strictly conserved; there is a pure natural source, from which guests are happily encouraged to drink.

Staff at the Estancia are acutely aware of recycling policies and routinely sort all solid waste. They also impart knowledge to guests in the course of nature walks and regular conversations about of a greener life.

This is a great place in which to discuss environmental issues because the benefits of green action can be seen.

Estancia Peuma Hue has been awarded the Eco Hotels of the World rating of 4 stars.

Address:
Road 40 - km 2014
San Carlos de Bariloche
Nahuel Huapi National Park
Rio Negro Province
Argentina

Telephone:
(+54-9-2944) 501030

Website:
www.peuma-hue.com

E-mail:
info@peuma-hue.com

La Cusinga Lodge

La Cusinga Lodge is a coastal rainforest eco-lodge dedicated to marine and terrestrial conservation and environmental education. Right on the South Pacific coast, the lodge provides guests with sweeping views of the ocean and marvellous flora and fauna. La Cusinga is part of a private nature reserve. Its guests have unparalleled access to Costa Rican wildlife such as morpho butterflies, tree frogs, ospreys, parrots, parakeets, toucans, howler monkeys, bottle-nosed dolphins, hawksbill turtles and the great humpback whale.

The reserve consists primarily of 250 hectares of virgin rainforest, bordering thousands of acres of privately protected forest. Several trails wind through the area and guests can indulge in anything from a three-hour trek to a stroll to the beach. There's something for all ages and abilities.

All the cabins at La Cusinga are comfortable and breezy with magnificent ocean views and beds for two or three people. Large groups can rent cabins with dorm-style accommodation, hot water and ocean views. All the cabins and rooms are crafted from trees grown on the property and are decorated by local craftsmen.

Rooms: 9

Ave. Rates: $135 USD

Activities: Rain forest hiking, Bird watching, Horse riding Canopy Observation platform, Surfi Nauyaca Waterfalls, Snokelling Dolphins an whales, Corcovado National pa Deep sea fishing.

★ ★ ★ ★ ★

La Cusinga Lodge has an up-to-date solar power system that provides electricity and heated water. Drinking and bathing water comes from a spring. The Lodge has its own recycling centre and promotes a new recycling program aimed at all the local hotels.

La Cusinga has a deep commitment to sustainability and development. This can be seen in the materials used to build it, and extends to concern for its environmental impact. It treats all waste material so that nothing harmful enters the forest, river or ocean.

Staff are all locals, and have devoted over ten years in some cases to developing this place and the promoting sustainable living through special events and seminars. La Cusinga Lodge is also something of a conservation success story. It promoted the creation of Ballena Marine National Park, one of the first places in the world where humpback from both the southern and northern hemispheres come to mate and give birth.

The lodge has been awarded the highest Eco Hotels of the World 5 star rating.

Address:
La Cusinga Eco Lodge &
Private Reserve
200 mts south of Km mark 166
Costanera Sur
Bahia Ballena de Osa
8000, Costa Rica.

Telephone:
506-2770-2549

Website:
www. lacusingalodge.com

E-mail:
info@lacusingalodge.com

Lapa Rios Ecolodge

S et in a private nature reserve spread over 1,000 acres of Central America's last remaining lowland tropical rainforest, Lapa Rios Ecolodge overlooks the pristine point where the Golfo Dulce meets the wild Pacific Ocean. Lapa Rios was built by John and Karen Lewis as a private nature reserve and matches many visions of paradise. A Minnesota couple driven by a vision, John and Karen liquidated all their assets to buy a large tract of rainforest and build a small supporting tourism project.

Today a conservation easement elaborated by The Nature Conservancy and Cederena ensure that this rainforest will be preserved forever. The Lapa Rios reserve is connected through a corridor with Corcovado National Park on the Osa Peninsula.

Lapa Rios is built in harmony with the surrounding forest and beach. The main eocolodge and bungalows are built along three ridges connected by walking paths and steps. Built over 350 feet above the sea, Lapa Rios catches cooling tropical breezes. The ecolodge, housing the restaurant and bar, soars fifty feet up and is built of local, natural materials. Palm-thatched roofs meet a three-story hardwood circular stairway that you climb to overlook the forest canopy and breathtaking ocean vistas. Relax in comfortable, locally made bamboo furniture surrounded by a tranquil panorama.

Rooms: 16

Ave. Rates:
On Request

Activities:
Horse riding
Sea Turtle tou
Dolphin tou
Hatha Yoga
Sunset birds t

W inner of five leaves from Costa Rica's prestigious Certificate for Sustainable Tourism (CST) and in the process of being certified as CNeutral, Lapa Rios has a rigorous conservation plan.

Its location, in a very remote area of Costa Rica (off the country's central electricity grid), has forced the owners to generate their own power. At the moment generators running on bio-diesel are sufficient although a feasibility study into micro-hydro might provide a better long term solution.

Solar panels supplement the hot water supply and a bio-digestor uses excess organic waste from the hotel kitchen to power the employees' kitchen. There are also pigs on the property, and methane gas from their faecal matter produces gas for the employees' kitchen stoves. Luckily water is plentiful but there is a linen and towel re-use program and staff training in water conservation.

Recycling is paramount and the ecolodge strives to reduce non-recyclable items from year to year. Lapa Rios works hard to educate guests on the importance of sustainability and to get them engaged with the local community. It offers local guided tours, including visits to farms and conservation projects, and promotional material about green ideas. Various projects in this area are supported by the ecolodge and guests can find out about them from a resident Sustainability Coordinator.

Lapa Rios ecolodge has been awarded the highest Eco Hotels of the World rating of 5 stars.

Address:
USA "Mail Drop"
Box 025216-SJO 706
Miami, FL 33102-5216

Telephone:
011- 506 - 735-5130

Website:
www.laparios.com

E-mail:
info@laparios.com

Le Parc aux Orchidées

U niquely here, guest bungalows have been built in amid one of the most significant orchid gardens in the world. Guests will find more than 450 different species of orchid and a thousand other plants. You have free entry into the park, with time to explore and photograph the gardens even outside normal opening times (when only guided tours are allowed). As a bungalow guest you get the place all to yourself.

There is a spa and swimming pool and few better ways to enjoy nature than from the side of a warm pool with a refreshing drink. The orchid garden was created by Jean-Claude Rancé. For thirty years he devoted himself to these magnificent plants and now Valerie and Richard Gautier continue his work. The garden boasts more than 3000 orchids and is among the largest collections in Guadeloupe. Add to this the thousands of flowers, palm trees, fruits tress and shrubs and you have a garden that could easily be mistaken for paradise.

Rooms:
2 bungalows
(self-catering
max 8 pers.

Ave prices:
2 Guests
43 to 92 €/nig
4 Guests
71 to 150 €/ni

Facilities:
pool, spa,
internet acce

I n this unique environment the conservation of the garden is a priority. The owners' care for the flowers translates into almost everything they do. Staff training means consumption is carefully monitored and targeted at reduction to zero carbon emissions in the next few years.

In the meantime a solar heater looks after water, and low light levels keep consumption low. Water is particularly valuable in a tropical rain-forest and the Parc uses only rainwater for irrigation. It endeavours to make guests eco-conscious and uses no harmful chemicals for cleaning.

Waste disposal, recycling and composting are brought to the attention of staff and guests. The Parc is also among the National Parks of Guadaloupe having been awarded a Marque de Confiance for conservation work.

As a member of the Botanical Conservatoire of the French Antilles its staff are involved in research into plant protection and have a practical understanding of healing plants. The Parc provides an incredible opportunity for those interested in plants and beautiful flowers to stay in a site of global importance.

Le Parc aux Orchidées has been awarded the Eco Hotels of the World rating of 4 stars.

 Address:
723 route de Trou Caverne
97116 Pointe-Noire,
Guadeloupe (FWI)

 Telephone:
+33 590 38 56 77

 Website:
www.parcauxorchidees.com

 E-mail:
contact@parcauxorchidees.com

127

Los Cardones

J ust one hour from Managua airport, Los Cardones is a premier surf destination in Nicaragua. The beaches are exposed to swells from both south-west and north-west, so the surf is consistent. Here you can hit the waves, get back and have a cold beer, eat a delicious meal, swap stories of your last outing at sea with the other guests, take a nap in the comfortable bungalows and then wake up to do it all over again. A true Nicaraguan experience.

There are five beachside bungalows, each with a private terrace, hammocks and lounge chairs. A spacious beach restaurant offers delicious food and more hammocks for relaxing afterwards. Other attractions include great fishing, snorkelling, horseback riding and nature exploration.

The lodge is family-owned and operated in the true spirit of ecotourism, striving to maintain a low environmental impact, promote conservation and a sustainable tourism that benefits the community.

Rooms: 6

Ave. Rates:
69$ per person
All inclusive

Facilities/Activiti
Surf, Boogie boar
Nature tours,
Horse back ridin
Day trips to
volcanoes,
colonial towns, a
typical marke
Every saturda
guests can joi
the art class a
the village sch

128

★★★★

Los Cardones is a fun, relaxed location that takes its ecological values seriously. Solar energy is used throughout and only the most essential items are hooked into the main grid. Water is pumped in from a private well and consumption is minimised as grey water is re-used in the garden. This saving is further strengthened by compost toilets.

Among the projects that operate here is Arte Accion, in which you can learn about the environment through art. Guests are invited to join workshops and participate in the community. There are some great nature trail tours and cultural tours including visits to pre-Columbian carvings.

Work in the community is important here. Everyone on the staff is a local and all supplies are bought from nearby producers. The spirit of conservation is strong, and as you enjoy the scenery and beautiful native garden, if you look closely you might just notice that not a single tree was cut for the building of this hotel.

 Address:
Km 49,
Carreterra Montelimar,
Pacific Coast,
Nicaragua.

 Telephone:
505 618 7314

 Website:
www.loscardones.com

 E-mail:
infoloscardones@yahoo.com

INTRODUCTION

Paradise Bay

E njoy dolphin and whale watching, catamaran sailing/ snorkelling, scuba diving, island tours, horseback riding, golf and hiking. Paradise Bay offers a serene holiday, local cuisine with a French accent, personal service, affordable massages and a gym. The resort is built over eight acres in an impressive natural park with fantastic ocean views.

Choose a suite with a Jacuzzi on the verandah and you'll be able to enjoy champagne by moonlight close to the ocean and the beach. All suites and rooms have a big bathroom and terrace, comfortable beds (one king-size or two singles), hardwood and rattan furniture and Italian tiles. Each resort suite has a small living room, which can sleep two on the sofa.

Rooms:
18 rooms/suite

Ave. Rates:
226 US$.

Activities:
Whale/dolphi
watching,
Catamaran tri
scuba diving
golf (9 course
horseback ridi
1-2 persons oc
kayaks, walks a
hikes; island to
massages an
other Spa
treatments
weekdays a
gymnasiun

★ ★ ★ ★

Paradise Bay's windmill was the first in the region and supplies 150% of the resort's energy. The management go even further by compensating the carbon emissions of all guests' flights and so guaranteeing a completely carbon-free vacation.

The site uses its own well and its collected rainwater: a great compromise between comfort and environmental protection.

Lately Paradise Bay has continued its ecological policy by installing advanced energy saving equipment such as air conditioning heat-recovery units. The Bay also promotes conservation to the local population by providing free seminars and 'environmental lunches' where guests get a free lunch when they buy energy saving light bulbs.

Paradise Bay has been awarded the Eco Hotels of the World rating of 4 stars.

Address:
La Tante, St David,
Grenada,
West Indies.

Telephone:
001-473-405-8888

Website:
www.paradisebayresort.net

E-mail:
info@paradisebayresort.net

The Pacuare Jungle Lodge

The Pacuare Lodge was built with a view to minimal impact on the river and rain-forest site where it is located. No trees were cut to build the bungalows and main lodge, and all the lumber was bought from a sustainable reforestation project operated by small farmers. Roofs are made from palm leaves laboriously installed by the local Cabecar Indians, who are experts in constructing the intricate traditional dwellings. Near the lodge, the owners have purchased nearly thirty hectares of ancient rainforest that was in danger of being cleared and have closed it to visitors, allowing it to continue developing naturally in perfect safety.

The Lodge operates a Community Support Program which works directly with the people and institutions of the Pacuare River. Infrastructure in these isolated areas is scarce and poorly maintained by the government so a percentage of each reservation made by internet is donated directly to the three primary schools along the Pacuare River between Tres Equis and Siquirres. A spirit of adventure and a true concern for the environment are just two of the driving forces for the staff at Aventuras Naturales, the company that owns the Lodge. The bilingual guides they provide embody the soul of this area and will even organise excursions to the wilds of Costa Rica's tropical rainforests, taking in beautiful pristine beaches and rivers along the way.

Rooms: 13

Ave. Rates:
On Request

Activities:
Canopy Tour,
Cabecar Indian
Day Break activity
Massage treatme

The Lodge has an excellent system for providing energy which combines solar panels for heating water with a small water-driven turbine. This eliminates any need for fossil fuels. Luckily there is ample supply of drinking water, which the Lodge also purifies further with an Acutab system. Staff are trained to use water responsibly and all cleaning products used are biodegradable. They all belong to one of three committees concerned with community development, waste management and training. They initiate new projects and chase improvements to the lodge's eco-sustainability.

Of the property's 260 hectares (639 acres), the bungalows and lodge infrastructure form 1% and the rest is tropical rainforest reserve. The Lodge grew out of the owners' desire to protect the site and stop it from going the way of so many other rainforest lands which have been deforested for farming or pasture. After eighteen years the work continues and the Lodge is involved in all manner of projects. These include a cultural calendar to highlight local Cebecar culture and community development ventures that repair roads and local infrastructure.

The Lodge is also an outstandingly positive force in wildlife conservation; it's a research centre for monitoring jaguars and a key site for re-introducing howler monkeys.

The Lodge has provided researchers with funds and facilities for studies that are, together with the environmental policies of the owners, helping to preserve the future of this natural paradise.

The Pacuare Jungle Lodge has been awarded the highest Eco Hotels of the World rating of 5 stars.

Address:
Turrialba,
Costa Rica

Telephone:
(506) 2225 3939
toll free from US
1-800-963-1195

Website:
www.pacuarelodge.com

E-mail:
info@pacuarelodge.com

The Tirimbina Rainforest Center

The Tirimbina Rainforest Center, or TRC, is a tropical science resource and eco-destination located within the rainforests of Costa Rica. Highlighting biodiversity, ecological systems, conservation and education, TRC offers eco-educational programs from grade school to university level as well as facilities for school groups, volunteers and researchers.

The rich rainforest environment around TRC provides a prime setting for exciting activities. Here you can hike the lush rainforest trails, discover wildlife, walk over swinging suspension bridges, or discover the secrets of cacao on the popular Chocolate Tour.

You can stay at Tirimbina Lodge near Sarapiqui river, surrounded by beautiful gardens, in one of fifteen comfortable airconditioned rooms with private bathroom, hot water, Wi-Fi, and phone; or the more adventurous can try the Field Station where two buildings afford close contact with nature. The Field Station is a fifty-minute trail hike from the TRC main offices and can accommodate up to forty people.

Rooms: 12

Ave. Rates:
$64 US tax and
breakfast includ

Activities:
Eco-education
activities,
Guided walks
Chocolate tou
Special bat
program,
frog tour
and night wa
Research
opportunitie
Volunteer
opportunitie
Access to th
forest by
suspension
bridges.

The Tirimbina Research Center is an exciting place where conservation and education are the main concern. Its mission is to promote understanding of tropical eco-systems and offer opportunities to research a biologically diverse environment.

Located within the rainforest and close to the river in Sarapiquí County, TRC is a private wildlife refuge. Its remit includes the protection of 345 hectares (852.5 acres) of mid-elevation forest. There are over nine kilometres (five and a half miles) of trails, full of wildlife for guests to enjoy, as well as exciting suspension bridges.

One third of the forest is used for eco-tourism and environmental education, and the rest is undisturbed. National and international students from elementary, high school and college visit TRC daily to participate in eco-education programs. Only last year, 6,000 students attended hands-on courses here and learned about ecology, biology, biodiversity and sustainable development.

The lodge is of course constructed in keeping with this environment. Electricity and hot water are provided by solar panels and the entire structure has been awarded the coveted Costa Rica Bandera Azul certificate for sustainable tourism.

The Tirimbina Rainforest Center has been awarded the Eco Hotels of the World rating of 4 stars.

Address:
La Virgen de Sarapiquí, Heredia
P.O. Box: 856-3000
Costa Rica

Telephone:
(506) 2761-1579

Website:
www.tirimbina.org

E-mail:
info@tirimbina.org

Active Holidays

What better way to enjoy nature than to be right in the middle of it, tasting the air, enjoying the view and feeling part of the countryside? Very few holidays can offer the level of freedom and enjoyment that an activity holiday can. You're are out in the open doing something new, different and usually enjoyable. Trips like these can have great benefits in a range of different ways.

Activity holidays lessen your impact on the environment. With transport representing the fastest growing source of greenhouse emissions, taking that element out of your trip in favour of a cleaner source of energy (your muscles) is will have positive effects.

Health benefits are tremendous. The more active people are, the less their risk of suffering from coronary heart disease, (obesity, stroke, diabetes, arthritis, osteoporosis and more. Walking and cycling are not only accessible, affordable ways in which people can reduce the risk of non-communicable diseases, but great fun. Besides, there's nothing so rewarding as a holiday dinner when you have had to work hard to get to it.

Cycling offers a good mix of speed and exercise and is popular with people of all ages. Global bicycle sales are at an all time high; more bikes than were sold in the US in 2008. In England alone people book around £120m worth of cycling holidays a year – or 450,000 trips.

Hiking lets enjoy the scenery at a slower pace and can take you the less-travelled paths. Or you could opt for a kayaking, climbing or even a swimming holiday. You still hear people talk about green travel as if it's a new idea, when activity holidays have existed for years.

Useful Contacts:

Escape Adventures
www.escapeadventures.com
Enjoy cycling tours, mountain bike trips and multisport adventures with Escape Adventures.

Adventure Collection
www.adventurecollection.com
A collection of sustainable tour operators and adventure travel companies.

The World Outdoors
www.theworldoutdoors.com
Outdoor recreation trips and adventure travel tours. Biking, walking, hiking and multisport vacations.

Country Walkers
www.countrywalkers.com
Offers walking tours, hiking vacations and snowshoein tours around the world.

Europe

Ard Nahoo

A rd Nahoo is an eco-retreat amid the unspoilt beauty of the North Leitrim Glens in Ireland, where it has established itself as a centre for alternative living and healthcare. You can book one of its innovative eco-cabins, timber-framed using only local wood and heated throughout by wood-pellet stoves, which are not only very fuel efficient but also give the warmest ambiance.

Within the grounds the choice of activities includes sessions in the Uisce area, with outdoor sauna and hot tub, yoga classes, holistic treatments, and organic food. Or you can just sit and relax in utopian calm.

Ard Nahoo is a convenient base from which to explore a charming area. Nearby you'll find hiking, surfing, horseriding, kayaking, caving and much more.

Rooms:
3 Eco Cabins
(7 rooms)

Ave. Rates:
Prices begin
at €190 for
two nights

Activities
Sauna, Steam ro
Jacuzzi, Yoga
Holistic therapi
Walks, Biking
Kayaking, Surfi
Swimming, Clim
Caving.

★ ★ ★ ★ ★

Holder of the EU Flower (a sign of the environmental quality of the property) and certified as an eco-retreat, Ard Nahoo has an excellent pedigree when it comes to providing holidays in harmony with the natural world. Its electrical power comes from Airtricity which operates wind turbines in Ireland and the UK. Hemp insulation and wood stoves ensure that the cedar-clad cabins are always warm and comfortable no matter what the weather outside is doing.

The eco-retreat collects rainwater so in the garden, thanks to a clever selection of endemic plants and of course the local weather, there is no need for irrigation. Recycling is also an important daily concern here and the retreat boasts its very own advanced recycling station. Guests help along with their own in-cabin recycling bins which are sorted by the staff. Organic material is composted for the vegetable patch which provides ingredients for the fabulous kitchens, where chef Maria offers delicious vegetarian dishes.

Ard Nahoo has been awarded the highest Eco Hotels of the World rating of 5 stars.

Address:
Mullagh,
Dromahair,
Co. Leitrim
Ireland.

Telephone:
+353 71 91 34939

Website:
www.ardnahoo.com

E-mail:
info@ardnahoo.com

Blizzard on fro▪
doorstep

Ashdene House

A dignified Edwardian guest-house offering Bed & Breakfast, situated in a quiet conservation area and located a mile south of Edinburgh city centre, Ashdene House has been owned and managed by the Daulby family for many years and their considerable experience is apparent in the quality of service and comfort provided.

There is unrestricted street parking outside the house and an excellent local bus service, with a stop just two minutes away, gives access to the city centre in ten minutes. Alternatively a stroll through the Meadows leads directly to the medieval Old Town.

Theatres, cinemas and restaurants are close at hand. There is a choice of restaurants within five minutes' walk; brochures and leaflets can be found in the bedrooms and at various other points in the house to help you decide. Tours are available around the city or to other parts of Scotland.

Rooms: 5
Ave. Price:
GBP49.00
p.p. per nigh▪
or
GBP99.00
p.r. per nigh▪
B&B
(includes fr▪
bus travel
throughout
Edinburgh
during stay▪

★★★★

Ashdene House has been accredited with the Green Tourism Business Scheme Gold Award. Its energy saving practices include the use of low energy appliances and lighting as well as comprehensive staff training.

Water is conserved through staff awareness and a linen re-use agreement with guests whilst wastage is reduced considerably by recycling. The hotel takes part in local activities and has a pro-active approach to local charities.

Ashdene House has been awarded the Eco Hotels of the World rating of 4 stars.

Front of House

Attractive walled garden

Address:
23 Fountainhall Road,
Edinburgh,
EH9 2LN,
Scotland.

Telephone:
0131 667 6026

Website:
www.ashdenehouse.com

E-mail:
res@ashdenehouse.com

Bedroom 1

Bedruthan Steps Hotel

Here in this picturesque corner of the north Cornish coast you can spend quiet sun-bleached days beside turquoise waves and soft sands. Tranquillity awaits you, punctuated by the occasional wild and spectacular storm. Bedruthan is a great place to explore hidden Cornwall and discover why so many are inspired by the natural landscape of the county all year round.

Bedruthan is a family owned hotel, cherished and nurtured over 48 years to give guests memorable holidays in a beautiful setting. All the rooms are simple and contemporary to reflect the hotel's architecture and beach-side location. They have huge comfortable beds, generous soft towels and all the extras that you would expect to find in a luxury four-star hotel.

Most bedrooms and all the guest areas boast spectacular views over the Atlantic Ocean. With twin, double and interconnecting hotel rooms, plus villa suites and extravagant apartments, there is accommodation suitable for all tastes and sizes of party.

Relax in the hydro spa with stunning sea views

Rooms: 101
Ave. Price:
From £67

Some of the Faciliti
Indoor pool
2 outdoor pools;
outdoor Jacuzzi;
Ocean Spa hydro p
Hammam room,
sauna, steam,
caldarium;
gymnasium;
onsite personal trai
snooker room;
2 tennis courts;
football pitch;
surf club;
table tennis;
table football;
air hockey;
'Jungle Tumble
funhouse for chilc
2 restaurants, ba
lounge and
poolside café

★ ★ ★ ★ ★

The Bedruthan Steps Hotel is a multi-award winning eco hotel with an incredible pedigree and an array of environmental policies from carbon footprint reduction to water and energy saving. All staff here receive an environmental induction when they join. They learn the details of Bedruthan's environmental practices, and managers are sent for external training. Energy and water saving features include key-card activated electrical systems, sensor-activated taps and dual-flush toilets.

Solar-heated outdoor pools

All cleaning products are organically produced and a written water-saving policy ensures consisten results for towel and linen re-use and guest awareness. The garden is irrigated by rainwater collected in a tank under the tennis-court. Staff and guests recycle everything, including some often overlooked items such as batteries, fabric, sun-loungers, mobile phones, CDs and printer cartridges.

When Bedruthan orders from suppliers, reduced packaging is requested, and it must be re-usable or recyclable - no polystyrene here! All garden and some kitchen waste is composted in seven compost bins. Bedruthan Steps made the pioneering move of being the first hotel in the country to employ a full time Sustainability Manager to coordinate their environmental initiatives. There is also a Green Team with a member from every department who meet regularly to discuss the hotel's sustainable progress. The hotel supports the local community by promoting local amenities and attractions, and by supporting the Cornwall Wildlife Trust, Surfers Against Sewage and the children's hospice. The hotel has adopted Mawgan Porth beach and staff and guests help to clean it four times a year providing data for the Marine Conservation Society. Bedruthan Steps Hotel has been awarded the highest Eco Hotels of the World rating of 5 stars.

Located above award-winning Mawgan Porth beach

 Address:
Bedruthan Steps Hotel,
Mawgan Porth,
Cornwall TR8 4BU.
United Kingdom

 Telephone:
(0044) 01637 860 555

 Website:
www.bedruthan.com

 E-mail:
stay@bedruthan.com

Can Martí

C an Martí is an oasis of calm in the north of Ibiza. The estate, which is more than 400 years old, and its four guest houses were built and restored according to ecological principles in the simple Ibizan architectural style. This has created a property that is elegant and also eco-friendly. The houses are spacious and cosy and guests immediately feel at home. Each house has its own outdoor space and feels private.

The estate has more than sixteen hectares of protected grounds, which guests are free to roam and explore. There is a working farm, which is run ecologically, with all sorts of things for guests to discover; for example, the new vegetable garden, which is based on the model of Gaspar Caballero de Segovia's Parades en Crestall, the aromatic herb garden, the hammam that is about to be opened and a farm shop selling homemade products and other organic items. You will soon make friends with the owners, other guests and even with the animals (donkeys, dog and cats).

Rooms:
3 studios for
1 cottage for

Ave. Rates:
Low season
130 € for tw
High season
160 € for tw

Activities:
Cycling, trekki
kayak, yoga
massages,
hammam,
pilates etc

144

C an Martí has made an effort to use the sun's energy as much as possible in the operation of its property. Photovoltaic panels and vacuum tubes supply about half the guests' electrical needs; 85% of all the power for hot water is solar. Guests are made aware of power wastage on their arrival and together with low-energy lighting and appliances help to make the houses extremely efficient.

Can Martí boasts low-flow showers and a rainwater collection system that runs from the roofs into a 25,000 litre cisterna (a pear-shaped underground container that almost all old Ibizan houses have). The overflow is channelled into an open tank that can contain about 160,000 litres and occasionally serves as a natural swimming pool. Grey water is passed through a biological purification system before running into a pond with fish, frogs and coots. Water from the pond is used for irrigation.

The property has an outside compost toilet which should be tried when visiting. Guests take an active part in recycling. The owners ensure that organic waste is turned into compost, food remains are given to the chickens and all other suitable waste is recycled. Can Martí is active in a number of social projects. 7% of its annual income is donated to international humanitarian organisations and locally the owners have created a small botanic garden with endemic plants for everyone to enjoy.

Can Martí has been awarded the highest Eco Hotels of the World rating of 5 stars.

Address:
Venda de Ca's Ripolls 29
Ctra de San Juan Km. 21
E-07810 San Juan - ibiza
Spain

Telephone:
+34 971 333 500

Website:
www.canmarti.com

E-mail:
info@canmarti.com

Can Martí

Eco Lives

The 400-year-old house, which once belonged to the well-known healer Pedro Torres Guasch, stood empty for a long time until the Brantschen family fell in lo with it and decided to restore it and make it their home. After 27 years of letharg during which only the sheep marked the passing seasons, the terraced fields were cleared, tree were pruned and old stone walls were repaired.

Inspired by permaculture, a mandala-shaped aromatic herb garden was designed. Later came organic orchard, which promised plenty of delicious fruit. The climax of the story came with arrival of Titane the donkey and her foal Sidi. Nowadays hens, cockerels and ducks share wit them the joy of living in this little oasis.

Chateau Mcely Club Hotel & Forest Retreat

C hateau Mcely is 55 kilometres northeast of Prague, in a state forest adjacent to the Jabkenice Game Park, famous for its magnificent walking and hiking trails. If offers 24 uniquely and exquisitely decorated bedrooms and suites, with single, twin and king-size beds.

In the Chateau you will find the world-class Alchymist Club Bar and Piano Nobile Restaurant. These feature a huge range of drinks, Czech and international wines, a fine selection of single malt whiskies and superbly prepared meals in a romantic setting. Although you can relax and unwind here, the hotel is also a high end business location, featuring a VIP Training centre for groups of up to fifty with teleconferencing, internet and audio-visual facilities.

All the rooms overlook beautiful parkland, and there is a relaxation centre, reflecting a holistic mind, body and spirit philosophy and staffed by experts in massage and therapeutic techniques.

Rooms: 24

Facilities/Activiti
Relaxation cent
Jacuzzi, Sauna
Massages

Croquet and
Pétanque,
Bicycles, Scoote
Excursions in
classic car, Hor
riding, Archer

Many offsite
activities includ
Golf, Tennis,
Bowling and
Clay-pigeon
shooting

I t's humbling to find hotel that is so luxurious and opulent that manages also to achieve formidable green credentials.

Legend Suite

Fulfilling European directive 43-2005 the Chateau has earned the coveted flower symbol making it the first 5* hotel in the Czech Republic, and the second in all Europe, with this classification.

Energy comes from wind power and hydro-electric plants and energy saving is achieved by ensured low-consumption electronic equipment and lighting and the watchful eyes of departmental managers.

The vast park is watered only with captured rainwater and recycled grey water, and guests are encouraged to use water efficiently. Waste management is important and a thorough recycling system is in place everywhere, including the guest rooms. Chateau Mcely is a founding member of the Microregion of St. George Forest.

This is an association of villages around St George Forest (Svatojirsky les in Czech) dedicated to safeguarding this complex woodland and its villages. Today's travellers will find tranquillity in this part of central Bohemia and will enjoy its cycling and walking trails and horse-riding paths.

Chateau Mcely has been awarded the highest Eco Hotels of the World rating of 5 stars.

Honey, Silk
& Pearls
Treatment

Address:
Mcely 61
289 36, Mcely
Czech Republic

Telephone:
00420 325 600 000

Website:
www.ChateauMcely.Com

E-mail:
Chateau@ChateauMcely.Com

Club Afrodit

C lub Afrodit is an unusual entry into our list as it is more than a hotel or lodge; it is a holiday village. It is surrounded by history, mythology and nature, with plenty of cultural treasures awaiting discovery nearby. Club Aphrodite (to use its English name) has a total capacity of 48 rooms, 23 Suites and eighteen Grand Suites. Since it can welcome up to 250 guests its efforts to be ecologically friendly are quite impressive.

Like any vacation camp there are activities for all the family: morning gymnastics, nature walks, tennis, ping-pong, aerobics, basketball, volleyball, darts, water polo and so on. Everything is available and for those in doubt there are team programs. Central to the wonderful outdoor space is a large pool, and if you're looking for even more fun in the sun there is a nearby private beach.

Rooms:
97 rooms
(48 hotel rooms,
23 Suites and
18 grand suites)
Maximum 250 Gue

Ave. Price:
50 euros

Some of the ma
activities/faciliti
available:

Tennis courts,
basketball, squa
fitness rooms,
sauna, massage
Turkish Bath,
swimming poo
private beach

This is one of the first such clubs in Europe to look at the environmental impact of running such a large property. Some of the techniques used to curb wasted energy and minimise harm to the environment are pioneering in a business of this kind.

Energy wastage is kept to a minimum and the rooms and indoor pool are powered by solar panels. There are sensor light installations throughout and rooms have the added benefit of fireplace heating. The most important aspect to conservation here is respect for the land, which stems from certification required by organic olive oil production.

This has affected everywhere, from the organic garden and vegetable patch to the lawn and native gardens, all grown with no insecticides or chemical agents and fed entirely by a recycled grey water system. Love of the land translates to the table where you will find plenty of produce from both this property and local villages and, of course, the famous olive oil.

Club Afrodit has been awarded the Eco Hotels of the World rating of 3 stars.

Address:
Altınoluk 10870 Edremit,
Balıkesir,
Türkiye

Telephone:
+90 (266) 378-0580

Website:
www.clubafrodit.com

E-mail:
afrodit@clubafrodit.com

The south end of the building from the pool area.

Ferme de Candeloup

In the foothills of the French Pyrenees, near the village of Monein, a 260-year-old Béarnaise farm has been transformed into a very special petit hôtel. At the heart of the Bearn region, it offers six charming en-suite rooms and a self-contained apartment, making it an ideal base from which to enjoy the area.

This is also a year-round yoga centre and retreat with a number of weeks dedicated to courses during the year; see the Ferme de Candeloup website. In winter, a forty-minute drive will take you to the nearest ski station, a short walk from the Spanish border. Whitewater rafting, horse riding and many other activities can also be pursued in the neighbourhood. For those of a more leisurely disposition, Candeloup is at the heart of the Jurançon wine region, which begs to be explored.

Rooms: 6 plus a ground-floor suit with disabled acce and facilities, all with private bathrooms.

Ave. Rates: Room-only prices start at 3 euros per person per nigh A large room with three peop would cost 75 euros includin breakfast.

Facilities: 10 x 4 metre (saline, not chlor swimming po

The key to the energy saving features of this property is in its insulation. The amount of insulation used is staggering; there are over five hundred kilos in the loft alone. The walls of the farm were 50cm thick to start with but they have been further insulated by the owners. Other features include low-energy lighting throughout, a clever arrangement of solar panels and an aerothermic system which extracts the heat present in the natural environment to provide hot water for guests.

Dining room, leading into the yoga studio/meeting room

The property is fitted with rainwater collection butts to a total of 3000 litres. This, together with well water, maintains the kitchen garden. The French location allows owners to be thorough about recycling, and guests are encouraged to pitch in; recycling bins are available to them. All organic waste is composted and as there is no main sewage system, the Ferme has an advanced fosse septique (septic tank) system with peat filter tanks.

The restoration of this old stone barn has been done with attention to detail and an eye to the environment. Even the furniture has been recycled, having been carefully collected in second hand stores and markets. Strenuous efforts are made to use food grown on site and what can't be provided here bought from the local market or, in the last resort, within the local region.

Courtyard and main entrance from the drive.

Ferme de Candeloup has been awarded the Eco Hotels of the World rating of 3 stars.

Address:
Chemin Augas
Quartier Candeloup
64360 Monein
France

Telephone:
0033 559 212 668

Website:
www.fermedecandeloup.fr

E-mail:
info@fermedecandeloup.fr

Room 1 looks out over the pool and the vineyards.

Hotel Tritone

Hotel Tritone is on Lipari, an island north-east of Sicily – one of the seven 'pearls of the Mediterranean', the Aeolian Islands, which are a UNESCO World Heritage Site. It is an elegant Mediterranean-style property overlooking the sea and features a wellbeing centre, swimming pool and hydro-massage pool with thermal water from a volcanic spring. The hotel provides a relaxing environment where you can sit back and enjoy a pool-side drink or walk through the beautiful garden, rich in local and tropical plants.

All this is only a few minutes from the centre of town and the Portinente beach. There are 38 rooms and a suite. All are soundproofed and have a private balcony or terrace – with a sea view on request. Luxury extends to the bathrooms where marble hydro-massage showers and bathtubs are standard size. In all rooms guests will find hairdryer and bathrobes, mini bar, satellite TV, SKY TV, internet, air conditioning and heating. The hotel has full disabled access. It offers fabulous meals in its elegant restaurant, serving Mediterranean and Aeolian cuisine à la carte with only the freshest Aeolian products.

Ave Rate:
Euro 70 in B&B
Euro 105 in HB

Facilities:
thermal outdoor
swimming pool
whirlpool, garden/p
à la carte restaura
bar in the lobby
conference room
40 sq. metres

Wellbeing centre w
sauna, turkish ba
hydromassage, sola
sport- oriental and
massages, beau
and other speci
treatments an
much more

★ ★ ★ ★ ★

Hotel Tritone has worked hard to achieve the ISO 14001 qualification, benchmark for the environmental qualities of a property. High-tech solutions have been applied throughout to ensure complete energy efficiency; every room is equipped with a master switch to ensure that guests don't leave their lights on. Low energy lighting as well as solar power completes the picture of a fairly large complex being run in an eco-friendly way.

All showers and taps have been installed with flow regulators, the toilets have a flush stop and a towel and linen re-use program is in place to ensure there is no unnecessary washing. Housecleaning employs only biodegradable detergents and in all rooms guests have information on how to save water. The swimming pool and hydro-massage pools use only spring water.

Packaging is strictly limited in all supplies bought by the hotel. This is particularly important since waste separation is not completely online in the island of Lipari until the end of 2008 (by which time the council here will begin to provide recycling bins). The staff are trained in ecological principles and they make sure, by means including guest awareness, that the property continues to run in the most efficient and green manner possible.

Hotel Tritone has been awarded the highest Eco Hotels of the World rating of 5 stars.

Address:
Via Mendolita
Lipari
Italy

Telephone:
+39 090 98 11 595

Website:
www.bernardigroup.it

E-mail:
info@bernardigroup.it

Iglu-Dorf

This is a unique entry in that it represents four distinct locations in Switzerland and one in Germany, all of which offer a similar experience and environmental standard. We have treated it as one entity but each village has its own unique character. They are:

Davos – Klosters (Switzerland)

The vacation paradise of the Grisons has much to offer with its splendid natural aspect and booming towns. Its people are deeply rooted in local tradition, but at the same time open-minded and cosmopolitan. Starting this winter an Igloo Village will be built in Parsenn Hauptertäli. A particular highlight is the sauna and whirlpool at 2,620m above sea level.

Engelberg-Titlis (Switzerland)

Surrounded by wild, romantic scenery in a wonderful location with breathtaking views of the Central Swiss mountains. Here in these igloos you can admire works of art created by real Inuit (Eskimo) artists. The Igloo Village in Engelberg can be reached quickly and easily from Lucerne, Zurich, Basel and Bern.

Gstaad (Switzerland)

Gstaad is in south-western Switzerland, bordering the French-speaking part of the country. The region can be reached easily by train from Lake Thun, Lake Geneva or the Gruyère area. The Gstaad Igloo Village is about 1,550 meters above sea level on the Eggli mountain near Gstaad. The view of the snow-capped Bern, Fribourg and Vaud Alps as well as the Gelten and Diablerets glaciers are a mountain lover's paradise.

Zermatt (Switzerland)

Zermatt lies at the base of the Matterhorn in the Valais Alps of southern Switzerland, 1.600 metres above sea level. You can get to Zermatt by train or taxi and from this incredible car-free town (in which carriages and cars are the main modes of transport) the Gornergrat railway will take you straight to the Igloo Village.

Zugspitze (Germany)

High above the clouds with a view of four countries lies the Zugspitze Igloo Village in the heart of Germany's most popular ski resort. Here you can enjoy the magnificent scenery of the Zugspitze Glacier and treat yourself to a very special night in Germany's most unusual accommodation.

★ ★ ★

These holiday villages share the same concept and environmental principles. The accommodation is unheated and relies purely on its design to maintain a constant temperature. LEDs and candles are used for lighting and the only significant power use is for the whirlpools and sauna.

There is no running water; guests have a water ration to last their entire stay, and there are neither washing machines nor flushable toilets. Drinking cups are marked at the beginning of the stay and are used by the same person throughout. As fondue is the main dish here there is little need for a variety of cutlery and plates, although those that are used are organic.

These igloos are a wonderful opportunity for guests to immerse themselves totally in the environment and enjoy fun activities like snowshoe walking, sculpting and even having a go at igloo-building.

Iglu-Dorf villages have been awarded the Eco Hotels of the World rating of 3 stars.

Address (Head Office):
Iglu-Dorf GmbH
Rotzbergstrasse 15
6362 Stansstad
Switzerland

Telephone:
+41 (0) 41 612 27 28

Website:
www.iglu-dorf.com

E-mail:
info@iglu-dorf.com

L'Ayalga Posada Ecológica

The owners of this beautiful house were determined to use only the best possible ecological materials they could, and their green principles can be seen in every detail of the building. Lime mortar allows the house to breathe, white cement instead of grey is free of slag from the blast furnaces, and wood has been treated with natural oils. Recycling, grey water systems, rainwater collection and solar panel heating add up to an energy efficient building that blends with its natural surroundings.

There are five guest bedrooms. Each is unique but all share the same level of luxury: latex mattresses, down-filled duvets and pillows, and 100% cotton bed linens and towels. Guests can enjoy relaxing activities including Tai-chi or Chi-kung lessons and massage.

In the library you will find books and magazines on ecology, human rights, healthy living and naturopathy besides the usual novels. If you feel like it you can also learn how to make fruit preserves, cleaning products or cosmetics using only natural products.

Ave. Price
Dbl Rooms
B&B 52.43 Eu
For one nig
B&B 58.85 Eu

Facilities
Private garde
music, librar
parking, gam
working far

★ ★ ★ ★

The home was constructed from the ground up with the environment in mind and this included natural materials for insulation. Water is heated by solar panels and all electrical fittings are energy-efficient. All rooms are fitted with showers rather than baths and with half flush toilets. A laundry scheme means towels and sheets are changed weekly unless guests request otherwise. Biodegradable products, some of which are made in-house, are used for cleaning.

The owners' concern for the environment is reflected in their involvement in breeding very rare Asturian horses. Information about local environmental and social initiatives is freely available. The farm is a patron of four main organisations concerned with human rights, ecology and underprivileged children. Guests are invited to make a gesture of solidarity by donating 1% of the price of their room to one of these worthwhile causes.

On a smaller scale, the farm buys only in the local market and guests are encouraged to visit local attractions, for example the museum of Porrua, or for Spanish speakers the Ruta del Queso y la Sidra (the cheese and cider route), the Museum of Asturcon (Asturian Horses Museum) or the Jardin de los Aromas (the Herb Garden). Staff encourage visitors to use public transport and provide timetables for trains and buses; they will also help you to plan journeys and tours.

L'Ayalga Posada Ecológica has been awarded the Eco Hotels of the World rating of 4 stars.

Address:
La Pandiella s/n
Piloña- Asturias
España

Telephone:
(0034) 985 710 431
Mob (0034) 616 897 638

Website:
www.terrae.net/layalga

E-mail:
layalga@terrae.net

Les Rayers

This B&B is in a nineteenth century bakery next to the main farmhouse. It has been carefully restored using ecological materials (natural paints and compost toilet, chemical and solvent free) and comprises a bedroom for two with adjoining bathroom and views over the garden. A delicious homemade breakfast is served in your room or outside in the morning sunshine.

The house sits in two hectares of land, and you are welcome to picnic in the field, chat to the chickens over your morning coffee, or watch the sunset whilst sipping a kir normand. If you don't feel like eating out, try our delicious evening meals. Scarlet and Ian do everything possible to make your stay enjoyable and relaxing. You will find a wide range of activities in the area: horse rides, hiking, biking, fishing, nature trips, courses, tour circuits, parks and gardens, listed buildings and the beautiful French countryside.

Rooms: 1
Ave. Price: 50

Facilities:
Barbecue,
picnic table,
tea-making
in room,
bike hire,
evening mea

In this idyllic French setting there is little need to remind guests to be respectful of nature. Here even the least sensitive will immediately pick up on the importance of environmental protection and the staff are only too happy to show some of the most important facilities they have installed as well as the advantages of living green. The whole property was upgraded to energy efficient and environmentally sound fittings including a compost toilet, which helps to save around 40% of water compared with a normal toilet.

Natural products are used in all cleaning, and grey water is recycled for the garden where techniques such as mulching minimise evaporation. All organic waste is composted. Garden waste that's too big for composting is left to rot naturally in a specially designated area: a big hit with insects and hibernating animals.

Some of the takings from the B&B go directly into a charity which has been set up in order to create an educational garden where people can learn about sustainable development, rural heritage and permaculture.

Scarlet and Ian also plant trees to offset carbon emissions and will happily do so on behalf of the guests (donations of 10 euros per tree). Guests can hire bikes to explore the area instead of using their car, and can ask for information on all the local highlights. The property is in the heart of a regional natural park, which is an area of remarkable cultural, historical and natural heritage. Les Rayers has been awarded the Eco Hotels of the World rating of 4 stars.

Address:
61400 Reveillon,
France

Telephone:
0033 (0)2 33 83 34 57

Website:
http://rayers.free.fr

E-mail:
rayers@free.fr

Levendis Estate

Levendis Estate is a 7-acre organic farm offering eco-chic, family friendly and romantic holidays on the shores of the Greek Ionian island of Ithaca. Perched on a hillside at the northernmost tip of the island, it's a working estate which has produced organic olive oil for four generations. Its grounds stretch from the shoreline up the hillside of a quiet wooded valley, providing the seclusion and privacy of a country estate with glorious views of the sea directly below, and villages within three kilometres.

Accommodation and facilities have recently been added. Four houses scattered throughout the groves provide good accommodation for the most discerning guest. Each is set within its own perfumed garden terrace. Sun-loungers in the shade of trees, along with a summer dining area on vine-clad terraces, take full advantage of the spectacular seascape.

Footpaths wander throughout the Estate connecting the houses with a morning coffee shop, organic herb and vegetable gardens, an outdoor cooking and refectory dining area, a separate farm area, an infinity pool with shaded colonnade, sun terrace and summer house, and on through a native forest where a holistic therapeutic massage pavilion is a secret waiting to be discovered. Hammocks and relaxation areas are in shaded glens. Elsewhere a small pebbled swimming cove lies just a ten-minute walk away through forests and groves.

Facilities/Activities

Infinity salt water poo
Morning breakfast/
brunch cafe,
Organic vegetable
gardens and orchard
Outdoor cooking
and dining area,
Holistic massage pavi
Farmyard animal ca
for children's participa
Child care - on reque
Cook - on request
Organic foods
prepared individua
Scuba diving,
marine biology exped
crewed yacht.

★ ★ ★ ★ ★

The Levendis Estate achieves a beautiful balance with the environment that is even more apparent when looking at the energy efficiency of the buildings. The position of the buildings and strategic planting in the grounds mean the eternal sea breeze cools everywhere to best effect.

Water is regulated three ways. A spring feeds directly to the houses, the pool is supplied by rainwater and the grounds are watered by a system of gravity-fed gravel pits. Sewage is taken away by a closed system to water the forests.

This efficient system keeps water use to a minimum. Levendis aims to leave as small a footprint on the environment as possible and enthusiastic composting and recycling mean even regular waste is thoroughly controlled.

The owners are currently applying for certification by the European Ecolabel Flower scheme.

Levendis has been awarded the highest Eco Hotels of the World rating of 5 stars.

Address:
Aphales Bay,
Ithaca,
Greece.

Telephone:
+30 6944 169 770

Website:
www.levendisestate.com

E-mail:
levendis@otenet.gr

How the Levendis Estate came to be...

One day in 1990 Marilyn Raftopulos and her family enjoyed a stroll in the land of her forefathers. As the hike grew into an a small expedition, and the roads narrowed to paths, it seemed that with every step they were discovering an ancient, mystical place where the work of previous generations had become merely an abandoned orchard of memories; yet where the trees quietly told a story for those willing to listen. A short six months later the land was theirs to protect and cherish. In the qui little spot where the children once played you will now find an incredible Estate. The trees st whisper stories and guide Marilyn on a journey to protect the fragility of this island paradise.

The swimming
pool at sunset

Locanda della Valle Nuova

This charming small country house lies in a 185-acre organic farm, within sight of Urbino which is a town on UNESCO's World Heritage list. It sits amid gentle, rolling hills, rich in wild flora and fauna, where ancient oaks are still protected as they were in the times of the Dukes of Montefeltro.

Bearing in mind that 'one should tread lightly on the earth', the owners grow their own organic wheat, fruit and vegetables and raise cattle, pigs and poultry with 100% natural feed. From their fresh produce they make their own bread and pasta, jams and wine and prepare traditional home cooking, all as flavourful as they are healthy. In autumn there are even truffles from the local woods.

Here the first priority is comfort: guest rooms are designed for a quiet stay and are both acoustically and thermally insulated. The house is fitted with solar collectors and the heating system uses only renewable energy, so as not to waste precious resources. Stables are available for those who bring their own horses.
Guests may swim in the magnificent pool with its sweeping view of the landscape or visit one of many nearby Renaissance towns.

5 dbl Rooms
1 Twin
2 Apartment
(2 people eac

Ave. Price
Rooms:
B&B 54 Euro
p.p.p.n.
Apartments
680 per wee

Swimming
Pool

Hiking
Trails

★ ★ ★ ★ ★

Although Italy has a flourishing network of properties near historic sites, Locanda della Valle Nuova is something of a rarity. Here the owners have not only looked at the importance of presentation and style but have kept a close eye on the environmental impact of the farm to ensure that the beautiful setting remains unaltered for future generations to enjoy. Nature is efficiently used, from the 15 hectares of wood that provide fuel for the high output wood-stoves, to rainwater for the big organic kitchen garden and solar power for heating water. Solar panels will be installed soon; in the meantime there is information in all the rooms on how to reduce energy consumption during your stay.

Take a rest in the shade in the company of the pure Marchigiana breed cows

The Locanda organically produces 70% of the food that is served on site the rest is bought directly from local producers, ensuring also minimal packaging. All the animals on the property (cats, dogs, hens and pigs) are fed with edible kitchen waste. Guests are invited to separate their waste and individual disposable toiletries are never used.

Home grown, home made organic breakfast

There is a concerted effort to reduce the farm's environmental impact by reducing waste and helping the grounds to remain a natural unspoilt habitat where the indigenous flora and fauna can flourish. Hunting is forbidden on this land and wild animals have made it a kind of idyllic oasis where nature and man coexist very happily.

Locanda della Valle Nuova has been awarded the highest Eco Hotels of the World rating of 5 stars.

Home made organic dinners

Address:
La Cappella 14
Loc. Sagrata
61033 - Fermignano
(Pesaro e Urbino - Le Marche)
Italy

Telephone:
+39 0722 330303

Website:
www.vallenuova.it

E-mail:
info@vallenuova.it

Old Chapel Forge

Old Chapel Forge prides itself on giving its guests the very best in comfort and service. The accommodation has been awarded a Four Star rating from the AA for five years in succession for high standards in service, cleanliness, food quality, and furnishings. The staff are also thrilled to have been awarded a Gold Award from the Green Tourism Business scheme for their environmental efforts.

Whether you are staying for business or leisure you will find the Old Chapel Forge gives you the location, tranquillity and comfort you need. To the staff at Old Chapel Forge, green tourism is not a product to be tagged on to a holiday; it is integral to the way the business is run. The aspiration and aim is to offer guests a 'green tourism' experience. Environmentally friendly alternatives are evident everywhere you look, whether it is the solar panels used for water heating or the use of organic and locally produced food only.

Rooms:
4 rooms all
ground floor
Ensuite with
both bath &
shower.

Ave. Rates:
Prices from
£25 - £55
per person
per night.

★★★★★

Old Forge Chapel has a total Green Build that has gained it an International Green Apple Award. A grey water recycling system is in place, waste is minimised in every way, and supplies are bought from local producers in re-usable packaging.

Guests are encouraged to take part in the hotel's green activities and this has allowed the staff to share their eco know-how.

Everyone at Old Forge Chapel is passionate about the local area and have even introduced a 'gift to nature' scheme that last year purchased sustainable cycle racks for the local nature reserve.

Old Chapel Forge has been awarded the highest Eco Hotels of the World rating of 5 stars.

Address:
Lagness,
Chichester
West Sussex,
PO20 1LR
England

Telephone:
01243 264 380

Website:
www.oldchapelforge.co.uk

E-mail:
info@oldchapelforge.co.uk

The Atami Hotel

The Atami Hotel is one of the finest boutique hotels in Bodrum, Turkey. This charming hotel, set in the undisturbed yet well-known Paradise Bay, is surrounded by breathtaking natural scenery, the perfect backdrop to some serious rest and relaxation.

Comfortable rooms and friendly service are provided by the Japanese-Turkish Oztaylan family.

The hotel has three suites, ten deluxe rooms and nineteen standard ones, each furnished with taste and attention to detail. The beach is just a few steps away and with just a snorkel you can marvel at what could easily be mistaken for an aquarium. If the local flora is more your thing there is a fabulous array of indigenous plants in the hotel's private garden.

If you tire of relaxing and swimming, you can choose activities from ikebana classes to yoga. Whatever you decid, this is a fascinating part of the country and an ideal place to look for some peace, intimacy and privacy.

Relax in the
Garden

Rooms: 32
Ave. Price: Euro 135

Safety Deposit
Boxes in Rooms
Mosquito Nets
Outdoor Restaura
Indoor Restauran
Pool Private Beach
Private Jetty
Mediterranean
Garden with
Relaxation Area
Pool Bar
Meeting room
(for 60 and for 1(
Squash Court
Table Tennis,
Wind Surfing Saili
Canoeing,
Ikebana lessons
Yoga Courses
Massage, Hikin
Special Interest Tc
Floating Marin
Internet Connec
Library Billiard & G

★ ★ ★

The Atami Hotel's rooms have energy saving devices as standard and in the cleaning department high-tech nano-technology reduces the use of chemicals.

For guests information cards suggest the option to re-use towels and bed linens and toiletries in the bathroom have been chosen for their minimal packaging. Staff are regularly educated about environmental concerns and the hotel's website reflects this with an entire section on global climate change.

The hotel hires local staff and in carefully selected local suppliers of tour and guiding services. It directs guests towards local businesses.

The Atami Hotel has been awarded the Eco Hotels of the World rating of 3 stars.

Lobby

Building

Pool Within the Garden

Address:
Cennet Koyu Cd.
N. 13 Golkoy,
Bodrum,
Mugla,
Turkey.

Telephone:
+90 252 357 74 16

Website:
www.atamihotel.com

E-mail:
info@atamihotel.com

171

The Hoopoe Yurt Hotel

The Hoopoe Yurt Hotel is set in three hectares of olives groves and unspoilt cork oak forest. Guests will enjoy spectacular views of the Grazalema mountains of Andalucia, in the rugged wilds of southern Spain.

You can choose between five styles of yurt. The Mongolian yurt is handpainted in burnt orange with traditional motifs in green, blue and gold. The Afghani one is more romantic, with bent willow poles and a deep red ceiling that make it cosy and intimate. The Jaipur yurt is made of coppiced chestnut and is light and airy, with dappled light filtering down through the cork trees. The Safari yurt is up at the top of the land with fantastic views over to Gaucin and Jimera, and is decorated in rich earthy colours. The Maimani yurt is also made of coppiced chestnut but with a closer lattice and more roof poles. The yurts are all set up as double rooms with comfy beds, traditional Mongolian furniture and exotic textiles. The camp runs on solar power and the yurts have overhead and bedside lights as well as sockets for charging mobile phones and laptops. They all have private bathrooms with hot showers and ecological loos.

Each yurt has an acre of private meadow with seating area, or you might prefer a hammock in the shade of the giant cork trees. Birdwatchers and botanists alike will find plenty to fuel their passion. The mixture of open meadow and forest provides the perfect habitat for dozens of bird species, and during the migratory months it becomes an ideal stopover for many more.

Rooms: 5

Ave. Rates:
2008
£95 / 120 euro
2009
130 euros

Activities:
Pool,
Mountain biki
Walking,
Birdwatchin
Massages,
Yoga,
Caves

★ ★ ★ ★

The most remarkable aspect of this property is that everything you see could be packed up and moved, leaving absolutely no mark on the land in which it is set. Energy and water conservation are high on the agenda and a mixture of clever grey water recycling techniques plus the composting toilets ensure that the gardens are immaculately kept.

The owners insist on local produce and buy in bulk to minimise packaging. Another great aspect of this accommodation is that guests are actively encouraged to take part in the life of the yurts and to learn about the measures in place to ensure an environmentally friendly existence. Each year work is done on clearing land in the surroundings to encourage the return of local wildlife. This, together with an effort to grow endemic plants has been a great success within the local ecosystem which guests will no doubt notice during their visit. The Hoopoe Yurt Hotel has been awarded the Eco Hotels of the World rating of 4 stars.

Address:
Apartado de Correos 23
Cortes de la Frontera
29380 Malaga
Spain

Telephone:
0034 660 668 241

Website:
www.yurthotel.com

E-mail:
info@yurthotel.com

Whitepod

Whitepod is an exclusive resort, unique and eco-efficient. Ten distinctive pods offer unusual and stylish accommodation at a camp that redefines Alpine living. Activities are available throughout the resort, including private ski trails opened just for guests, night and day.

Far away from the crowds, yet providing the highest standards of comfort and service, Whitepod is unforgettable. 1,400 up, the award-winning camp consists of ten Pavilion pods and a main lodge. The pods are suites, fifty metres square, with bathrooms and lounge areas. There is also a spa pod with treatment rooms and a hot tub which can be booked exclusively.

Each pod serves as a bedroom, designed for double or single occupancy, except for the Group Pod which sleeps up to eight. Heated by a wood burning stove and insulated with the latest technology, they are wonderfully warm day and night.

Rooms:
10 Pods

Ave Rates:
585CHF
per night per
(for two),
including brea
and all taxe

W hitepod is an incredible achievement, a luxury resort that manages to offer extraordinary comfort on the mountain slopes yet remains in harmony with its surroundings. Here as the snow settles on the domes, everything becomes part of the landscape and you almost forget the considerable effort that has gone into making the camp ecologically super-efficient.

Environmental impact is minimised as strict regulations on water and power use, as well as waste disposal have been put in place by caring staff. They willingly show guests their energy saving techniques and explain the best local products and services.

Whitepod's principal goal was to offer an alternative to increasingly overcrowded (and non-eco) ski resorts. The target has been surpassed in every way.

Whitepod has been awarded the highest Eco Hotels of the World rating of 5 stars.

 Address:
Les Cerniers
1871 Les Giettes
1871
Switzerland

 Telephone:
0041 24 471 38 38

 Website:
www.whitepod.com

 E-mail:
info@whitepod.com

Carbon Offsetting

A few years ago the idea of carbon-offsetting was beginning to catch on. As people started to develop an eco-conscience (and the resulting eco-guilt) the prospect of suddenly not having to worry about their carbon footprint any more was incredibly appealing. Since then, scores of businesses have appeared, promising the world that we could simply buy ourselves out of our troubles.

Unfortunately the truth, as is so often the case, is a little more complex. The idea is simple. In theory, the carbon you produce can be offset somewhere else in the world by paying into a project that will reduce the same quantity from the atmosphere. At the beginning, schemes tended to concentrate on planting new trees since they sequester a certain amount of CO_2 during their lifespan.

Today they are more social and energy-based. The most modern schemes use the money in developing countries to do a number of things including installing energy efficient lighting and appliances. These do have educational benefits for the receiving communities.

In theory, then, it's an excellent way to offset the inevitable carbon footprint we all create. However, there are considerable difficulties with carbon offsetting. First of all, it is merely an interim solution that only temporarily buys us out of the problem. It doesn't address the causes of carbon emissions, or show us how to reduce them. We should first look at ways to reduce carbon production. More practically: if I were travelling from London to Paris with a choice between train or plane, should I pick the train to reduce my emissions and support a more environmentally friendly service, or pick the flight and offset it? The right solution is the train; the plane is just a quick-fix option. Our lives need to be conducted in an environmentally friendly way before we think of offsetting anything. Lastly, all schemes are not equal. If you must offset, do some research to find one that you know has had good results in the past. You don't have to accept automatic offsetting options on websites if you feel more comfortable with a supplier you know.

Useful Contacts:

The CarbonNeutral Company - www.carbonneutral.com
One of the leading carbon offsetting provider for over 10 years, offering a wide range of carbon offset projects

Blue Ventures Carbon Offsett (BVCO) - www.bvco.org.uk
A not-for-profit carbon offsetting programme helping communities by investing in carbon management projects with practical benefits.

North America

Alaska's Ridgewood Wilderness Lodge

Soak up the Alaskan wilderness at this intimate, timber framed lodge on Ishmailof Island adjoining Kachemak Bay State Park, part of the Kenai Peninsula Mountain Range. Enjoy three gourmet meals a day, highly personal attention with majestic scenery, miles of beaches, and secluded saltwater coves right outside the front door.

The hosts of this secluded getaway are two sourdough Alaskans, Kevin and Lucinda Sidelinger. Kevin, who built the lodge using timbers from the Pacific Northwest and Alaska, created a building that complements the environment.

The Douglas fir, timber-framed bedrooms offer plenty of space as well as large windows and panoramic views of the bay, mountains, and beaches, along with private baths and an undeniably Alaskan flavour. Or indulge your senses watching for whales, porpoises, sea otters, and seals from the decks that surround the lodge.

Rooms: 4
2 rooms with one queen sized bed in eac
1 suite with one queen sized bed and a queen sized sleeper sofa
1 room with a set of bunk beds for singles or children. Can accommodate up to 10 people. Rooms have private baths

Ave Lodge Price: $350.00 per day, per person, year 'round. (no peak season)

Facilites/Rates Inclu
3 gourmet meals per day, compliment
housekeeping and
laundry facilities,
high-speed
wireless internet

★ ★ ★ ★ ★

Alaska's Ridgewood Wilderness Lodge was the result of a careful plan to produce a building with minimum footprint and minimal energy requirements. At the design stage its creators took into careful consideration every single detail, from the location (picked not only to take advantage of the panoramic view but also the passive solar gain from the long days in the Alaskan summer) to the layout (dictated by vegetation in a bid to remain in perfect equilibrium with the environment) and even in the choice of materials and fittings.

The Lodge has worked hard at taking every conventional problem and solving it with a view to guest comfort and low or no environmental impact. Experts were drafted in to produce acceptable systems of disposal particularly for water-borne waste, where a state of the art Bio-Cycle system was designed to treat all waste water biologically.

At Alaska's Ridgewood Wilderness Lodge, guests are informed of the eco-philosophy behind this beautiful building and this information also helps in maintaining a low footprint from visitors to the wilderness area. The owners of this Lodge really took every component to its basic design and helped define what an eco-lodge in Alaska would be, even before there was a name for it. This philosophy is a part of their everyday lives and has become the core value in the operation of the Lodge and their nearby oyster farm, considered by the Alaska Department of Environmental Conservation as a valuable addition to the local ecosystem. Alaska's Ridgewood Wilderness Lodge has been awarded the Eco Hotels of the World rating of 5 stars.

 Address:
P.O. Box 659
Homer,
Alaska 99603
USA

 Telephone:
(907)296-2217

 Website:
www.ridgewoodlodge.com

 E-mail:
ridgewoodlodge@homernet.net

Alaska's Sadie Cove Wilderness Lodge

Alaska's Sadie Cove Wilderness Lodge is on a remote privately owned beach inside Kachemak Bay State Park, midway between the villages of Seldovia and Halibut Cove, and only ten miles by boat from Homer, Alaska, bear-viewing capital of the world. The Lodge was custom built in the mid 1970s from driftwood individually handmilled by the owner, Keith Iverson. Accessible only by boat, float-plane or helicopter, Sadie Cove Wilderness Lodge offers a unique opportunity to participate in Alaska's wilderness lifestyle with a couple of true Alaskan sourdoughs.

The early Alaskans camped here seasonally to make stone tools and gather berries, clams, mussels, seals, and sea birds for subsistence. This historic link was recognised by anthropologists who explored the bay in the 1940s and found ancient middens and cave paintings on what is now Lodge property. Today, to retain the peaceful atmosphere of the wilderness and to maintain the ecologic sustainability of the land, Sadie Cove Wilderness Lodge serves a small number of overnight guests only.

Additional patrons are never brought in for meals, equipment rentals, the Lodge's signature eco-tours, or sales of any kind. Here the small guest capacity and the non-commercial, homey atmosphere will give you time and space to feel comfortable and form new friendships.

Rooms:
5 Private Cabins.

Ave. price:
$400 per night.

Facilities:
Privately owned bea
inside Kachemak
Bay State Park, Alas

Free use of kayak
and fishing gear
Private hiking,
log cabin sauna
with plunge poc
Bear tours, whal
watching, birdin(
local village tou

Private parties o
or more get th
entire lodge to
themselves an(
the maximum
guest count is 1

The award-winning Sadie Cove Wilderness Lodge has all the modern comforts we've come to expect yet manages to exist in complete harmony and respect with its rugged and unharmed surroundings. The building is off the electrical grid and power comes either from a hydroelectric generator fed by the mountain stream, or from a wind power generator.

The Lodge has a written energy use policy and recycling stations, and employees are educated in all aspects of energy and water conservation. Due in no small part to its location, the Lodge has always recycled and further use is often found for products that would otherwise be dumped. For instance, used plastic pipes from a defunct salmon hatchery were reborn as roof gutters, old milk containers became plant pots, and kitchen refuse is always re-used for composting.

The Lodge was benchmarked by Green Globe Alaska Department of Environmental Conservation for a Green Star Award. It hires only local Alaskan guides and staff. Produce is grown in the grounds and supplemented from the local farmers markets. All dry goods are purchased in bulk to reduce the enormous amounts of packaging that would otherwise present a recycling challenge. Everything on the property is done in a way that our Alaskan forebears would approve of.

Sadie Cove Wilderness Lodge has been awarded the highest Eco Hotels of the World rating of 5 stars.

 Address:
In Kachemak Bay
State Park Box 2265
Homer,
Alaska.

 Telephone:
907-235-2350

 Website:
www.sadiecove.com

 E-mail:
mail@sadiecove.com

Algonquin Eco-Lodge

T he Algonquin Wilderness Eco-Lodge, located on the southern border of Algonquin Park only three hours from Toronto or Ottawa, is a wilderness enthusiast's dream. Summer or winter, there is always plenty to do and see. With over 60 kilometres of groomed track and wilderness trails inside Algonquin Park, the Algonquin Eco-Lodge is a leader among hotels for cross country skiing, dog sledding, hiking, canoeing, and mountain biking. Designed and built as an Algonquin Nordic Wilderness Lodge, the Ecolodge was created to give the best wilderness experience possible, while minimizing its impact on the environment.

It has the feel and atmosphere of a European mountain lodge, and is one of the most secluded hotels in Algonquin Park. The experience begins with a leisurely mile-long walk, or cycle, or ski through Algonquin Park to reach the front door. (Don't worry - your luggage will be transferred for you.)

Even hydro lines and telephone poles can't reach this secluded spot in the Algonquin forest; yet, with a combination of alternative energy sources, the Eco-Lodge provides every comfort. You will find indoor plumbing, battery-powered hot showers, an outdoor wood-fired sauna all year round, and even a hot tub for use in the cold winters. With seventeen private bedrooms, there is more than enough space for 34 guests.

Rooms: 15

Ave Rates:
$125/person/nigh
in the summer,
$140/person/nigh
in August.
Meals are include
10% taxes and
5% gratuity is ext

Facilities:
2 shared bathroo
free use of canoe
and paddle boat
hiking trails, saur
private lake,
bonfires, free park
free transfer
of luggage.

★ ★ ★ ★ ★

Algonquin Wilderness Eco-Lodge takes its power from a newly installed micro hydro-generator installed on its waterfall. Water for consumption comes from a well and waste water is processed by a septic tank on-site. Low-flow WCs and showers have been installed throughout as well as ample signs to encourage minimum water usage.

All paper, plastic and metals are recycled and guests are encouraged to minimise their waste. Composting is unfortunately impossible due to the presence of bears. The Lodge is also involved in maintaining fort-five miles of wilderness trails, and encourages guests to take day trips by canoe. Guests are directed to local artists and shops and all supplies and services come from local businesses.

The Lodge has been awarded the highest Eco Hotels of the World rating of 5 stars.

 Mailing Address:
Algonquin Eco-Lodge
23 Edward St.
Markham, ON
L3P 2N9

 Telephone:
905-471-9453

 Website:
www.algonquinecolodge.com

 E-mail:
EcoLodge@CallOfTheWild.ca

At Kw'o:kw'e:hala eco retreat

At Kw'o:kw'e:hala eco-vacation retreat is next to the breathtaking Coquihalla Canyon Provincial Park and Othello Tunnels of the old Kettle Valley Rail. This eco-retreat is located away from the masses on seven forested acres alongside the emerald waters of the Coquihalla River.

The stunning wilderness around the lodge is the perfect setting in which to relax, play, eat and sleep. There are cosy forest cabins, private riverside lounges, a beach, and a natural outdoor spa with a wood-fired cedar hot-tub and an authentic Finnish sauna.

Mouthwatering cuisine, made from the fresh organic garden and other local sources, is served in the outdoor dining-room by the river. Everything at the lodge is designed to give you a natural adventure full of balance, comfort and fulfilment. The location, away from the stress of urban life, completes the experience and will leave you in a state of peaceful relaxation.

The Nest: private riverside lounging

Rooms:
3 cabins
Ave. Rates:
$125 per person
all inclusive

Activities:
Eco retreat, Natur
Hiking, Cycling
Gourmet food,
Organic garden
Fine wines,
Wood-fired hot t
Wood-fired saun
Relaxation,
Riverside Nes
accommodatio
Government Pa
Coquihalla Riv

★ ★ ★ ★ ★

Every aspect of conservation in this eco retreat is carefully thought-out and amazingly efficient. The site employs natural light, solar light, kinetic light and biomass for most of its heating with minimal use of on-grid electricity (80% of which is hydro-produced).

Wood-fired hot tub in the forest

As the retreat is located in a coastal rain-forest there is a careful system of water management starting with an on-site well and with an environmentally conscious waste-water biological system that recycles 100% of human water waste.

This minimum impact policy extends to wastage where a well-run recycling program ensures no impact on the environment. Everything possible is re-used and the rest is sorted and recycled.

Riverside dining room - delicious organic cuisine

The eco-philosophy of the retreat has been fine tuned by decades of experience. A number of green-minded beneficiaries are supported through donations and education is freely given to guests who want to learn more about becoming eco-aware. The retreat is socially responsible, buying most supplies locally, supporting organic farmers, and helping to maintain local hiking and cycling trails.

Local contractors make up 100% of staffing needs, and the retreat is a committed member of WWOOF, a volunteer network of willing workers on organic farms.

At Kw'o:kw'e:hala eco vacation retreat has been awarded the highest Eco Hotels of the World rating of 5 stars.

Relax by the river

Address:
67400 Tunnels Rd.
Hope, BC, Canada
V0X 1L1

Telephone:
1-877-eco-retreat (Toll free USA)

Website:
www.eco-retreat.com

E-mail:
info@eco-retreat.com

Best Western Kamloops

This hotel was recently upgraded to include a geothermal system, a natural chlorine pool and a new lobby and south wing. Free high-speed internet and working desks are available in all rooms. In addition, the 203-room hotel features an indoor tropical courtyard with a pool and kids' wading pool. Among other amenities, there are deluxe rooms and suites, an Aberdeen Liquor Store and a 30,000 square foot conference centre.

To complete the experience there is one of the finest restaurants in Kamloops, overlooking the courtyard Forsters Restaurant and Spirits Lounge. In this area you will find some of the finest golf courses in the country, horse riding, mountain biking, hiking, fossil exploring, and Western Heritage. If you are more of a winter person then nearby you have the excellent ski Sun Peaks Resort, which is quickly becoming one of the premier ski areas in Canada.

Rooms: 203

Ave. Rates:
$125 - 175

Activities
Golf,
Sightseeing
Skiing, Fishing
Sports, Events
Conference
Corporate

★ ★ ★

The Best Western Kamloops is a 3 Green Key Property as recognised by the Canadian Hotel Association; it's also a member of the Green Hotel Association. In 2005, as part of a major refurbishment program, there was heavy investment in a geothermal heating and cooling system which has reduced their gas requirements by 50%. Solar panels also provide energy from a natural source.

Cardboard, bottles and all internal paper are recycled. Old sheets and towels become re-usable rags or are made into storage bags. Dispensers have been fitted in all rooms, and this apparently minor change alone has removed 128,000 small bottles of shampoo and soap from landfill every year and reduced toiletry waste by 40%.

The hotel, as an important local buyer, has been able to pressure its suppliers into taking a more eco-friendly approach to their business and insist upon sourcing things locally to further reduce their carbon footprint.

The Best Western Kamloops has been awarded the Eco Hotels of the World rating of 3 stars.

Address:
1250 Rogers Way
Kamloops, BC
V1S 1N5
Canada

Telephone:
250-828-6660

Website:
www.bestwesternkamloops.com

E-mail:
info@bestwesternkamloops.com

Cedar House Inn and Yurts

Experience the ambience and feel of a mountain lodge just seventy minutes north of Atlanta. Located near the base of the Appalachians, at the heart of the north Georgia wine country and home of the nation's first Gold Rush, this rustic but charming B&B provides a refuge from city life. You can settle into the Cardinal Suite or one of the two cosy rooms with knotty white pine walls, queen-size beds, private baths, and private entrances opening onto quiet patios.

Or, you can choose between two yurts. Their canopied queen-size beds and simulated wood stoves offer a romantic ambience. Located just five and a half miles north of the historic public square of Dahlonega, Cedar House is convenient for all the mountain attractions. The Appalachian Trail and other hiking areas are just minutes away Amicalola Falls, DeSoto Falls and several other waterfalls are nearby and offer great hiking opportunities. Alpine Helen, the historic Sautee Nacoochi Valley, and Unicoi State Park are just over a half hour's drive east. For active guests there is horseback riding, kayaking, canoeing, or tubing down the Etowah or Chestatee Rivers. Whether you love mountain biking on rugged trails, or road biking, you can sample some of the local routes, often used by professional racers.

Rooms:
3 rooms, 2 yurts

Ave. Rates:
vary to season,
low is $85.00
per night per roo
high is $125.00
per night for suit

Breakfast include

Activities nearb
hiking, biking,
waterfalls,
wineries, shoppi
antiquing, tubin
kayaking on riv
fishing for trou
Appalachian Tr
community thea

On site facilitie
common living a
outdoor patic
for viewing
birds/nature

★★★★

edar House Inn and Yurts has taken great care to install only energy-efficient lighting and appliances. There is an advanced insulation system and wood stoves to minimise energy usage. The staff are well trained and can educate guests on saving electricity and the impact this has on the environment. There is a concerted effort to plant only indigenous species and although grey water recycling is illegal in Georgia, the Inn does a great job of collecting rainwater and using showerheads and sink aerators which, coupled with the composting toilets in the yurts, make the property water efficient.

There is a green cone and drum composter on site and the management's policy is not to buy disposable, favouring recyclable items. Recycling continues in the guest rooms where bins are provided as well as information on why to use them. Eco-friendly charities are given free room nights and eco-education is firmly in place thanks to the written information available to all guests, as well as discussion time during morning and evening visits.

The Inn encourages guests to visit local businesses and the local CSA (community-supported agriculture) farm and strawberry farm, the nearby wineries and National Forest areas.

Cedar House Inn and Yurts has been awarded the Eco Hotels of the World rating of 4 stars.

Address:
6463 Highway 19 North,
Dahlonega,
GA 30533
USA

Telephone:
706-867-9446

Website:
www.georgiamountaininn.com

E-mail:
info@georgiamountaininn.com

Inn by the Sea

Ocean view Lobby at eco luxury Inn by the Sea

A multi-million dollar makeover has elevated the Inn to become Maine's premier luxury beach destination. New services and amenities have been added, changing nearly everything except the warm and friendly staff. All 57 guest rooms, suites and cottages have been designed to pamper, with their a sophisticated palette of deep red, cognac and charcoal, maple furnishings and locally commissioned artwork.

The Inn offers a full-service Spa where you can unwind and be soothed by luxurious facials, massages and treatments. And, while you gaze at the spectacular beauty of Crescent Beach, the restaurant Sea Glass presents authentic Maine food prepared from the freshest local ingredients.

The Inn is eager to welcome guests and continues to uphold its environmentally sensitive and pet welcoming practices. It's only minutes away from Portland, named among the top twelve surprising, thriving and emerging world travel destinations for 2007 by Frommer's Travel Guides.

Rooms: 57 rooms, suites, and 2 bedroom condo suit●

Amenities:

3 miles of sandy Bea
Ocean view restaura
private dining room
Wine cove
2 Function rooms
Fireplace bar and lou
Outdoor dining
5 acres garden
Private boardwalk to b
heated pool spa,
cardio room,
outdoor fire pit
boule, croquet &
lawn games
golf and boating ne●
canoe and kayak
in nearby nature pres
10 minutes to Portla
historic Old Port

I nn by the Sea enjoys superb surroundings in which it's easy to miss how much effort has gone into ensuring that its ecological credentials are up to the highest standard. Energy saving is paramount, and all fittings are low-energy and controlled with timers. This hotel is also the only one in Maine heated with biofuel (soy mix) whilst the swimming pool is heated by solar panels.

Children and pets both pampered at Inn by the Sea

There are regular classes on all conservation matters and on planting in the five-acre garden of indigenous species. There are towel programs and recycling bins in all rooms and in communal areas other touches include a recycled rubber floor in the cardio room and recycled studs and recycled sheet rock in the spa. Staff attend regular meetings about eco-matters; bulletins deliver information to all guests and the Green Program manager, Rauni Kew, is a regular lecturer on sustainable business.

The Inn is committed to local suppliers and only the freshest ingredients make it to Sea Glass restaurant, thanks to Chef Kaldrovich's farm-to-table principles.
Inn by the Sea has been awarded the highest Eco Hotels of the World rating of 5 stars.

Sandy Crescent Beach

Address:
40 Bowery Beach Road
Cape Elizabeth
Maine 04107
USA

Telephone:
207-799-3134

Website:
www.innbythesea.com

E-mail:
info@innbythesea.com

Inn Serendipity

A visit to Inn Serendipity is more than a typical night's stay at a Bed & Breakfast. At Inn Serendipity®, the owners have created a magical, creative environment where you can play, explore, create, relax, learn . . . and return home with a refreshed perspective on life. Sketch under the willow tree, philosophise around the campfire, enjoy a hearty vegetarian breakfast with organic fruits and vegetables from the Inn's gardens, or lose yourself in a book from the eclectic library. Open your soul to serendipity and relish the abundance and spirit of all life.

Entirely powered by wind and sun, the award-winning Inn Serendipity Bed & Breakfast in south-western Wisconsin features hearty, seasonal vegetarian breakfasts mostly prepared with ingredients from the Inn's organic gardens. Recognised as one of the top ten eco-destinations in North America by Natural Home and featured in USA Today, ABC News and the New York Times, the Inn is also the setting for the innkeeper-authors' books. Lisa Kivirist and John Ivanko have written ECOpreneuring, Rural Renaissance, and a cookbook, Edible Earth.

Inn Serendipity® Bed & Breakfast featuring perennial gardens and a solar thermal system that heats the guests' shower water by sunlight.

Rooms: 2
Ave Price:
$105 - $120

Amenities:
guest library,
life-size chess set,
campfire area,
perennial gardens

I nn Serendipity is spearheading ecological awareness thanks largely to the expert guidance of its keepers, who have the good fortune to be successful authors at the forefront of teaching others the advantages of a greener life.

The Inn's wind and sun power generates a surplus of more than 1,000 kilowatt hours, sold back to the utility grid. The energy savings extend beyond the building where an electric CitiCar is recharged by an off-grid solar electric system.

Several water catchment systems ensure water conservation. Advanced recycling practices include the re-use of waste materials from the community in its business operations. The key at Inn Serendipity is education, and what better teachers than Lisa and John, who will take you on an engaging complimentary tour of the farm and its renewable energy systems. Afterwards you can sit back and relax with one of their books while sipping lemon balm iced tea and enjoying the sights and aromas of the kitchen garden and perennial flowers.

Off-grid PV system that recharges all-electric CitiCar

Inn Serendipity has been awarded the highest Eco Hotels of the World rating of 5 stars.

Innkeeper-authors' books

Address:
7843 County P, Browntown WI, 53522,
USA.

Innkeepers-authors. Lisa Kivirist and John Ivanko

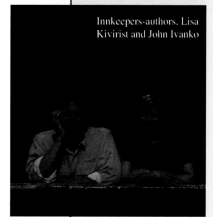

Telephone:
608-329-7056

Website:
www.innserendipity.com

E-mail:
info@innserendipity.com

The Sustainable -- and Serendipitous -- Journey at Inn Serendipity

After several years navigating the cubicle maze, helping to sell products of questionable value for either people or planet, John Ivanko and Lisa Kivirist departed corporate America on a journey to create a new livelihood, in a way that express their passion to make this world a better place. Letting the sense of place serendipitously seep in -- from the foods they serve from Inn Serendipity's organic gardens to the wind and sun use to power the farmstead -- they've discovered that the good life has little to do with the goods life. After over a decade of living more sustainably, they've discovered their emerald-coloure pot of gold at the end of the rainbow and enjoy the diversity of guests who share their vision a more peaceful, just and ecologically-based future.

Lookout Point Lakeside Inn

Lookout Point Lakeside Inn is an exceptional Bed & Breakfast in Hot Springs, Arkansas. Nestled in the Ouachita Mountains overlooking a tranquil bay of beautiful Lake Hamilton, Lookout Point represents a sanctuary for body and soul.

Here you can enjoy unparalleled luxury, personal pampering, relaxation, superb hospitality and privacy and take time off to have a swim in the lake, snuggle by the fireplace, canoe the bay or even walk the labyrinth. There are hiking trails in the Hot Springs Arkansas National Park as well as Lake Ouachita and Lake Catherine State Parks.

Nearby you can soak in the thermal mineral waters of America's first Spa City. Indulge yourself with hearty, fresh breakfast and afternoon refreshments and end the day with a great sleep in a luxurious bed with fine bedlinen. The Inn's motto: relax, rejuvenate, restore.

Rooms: 12

Ave. Rates:
On Request

Activities:
Canoeing,
Parasail,
Water ski,
Duck boat to
Hot Springs
National Park
Lake Catherine
State Park

Lookout Point Lakeside Inn's environmental policy covers all major aspects of conservation: energy, water and waste disposal. Energy is coserved by excellent modern insulation and thorough training of staff who ensure there is no wastage.

The nearby lake, which also feeds the on-site fountain, is an ever-present reminder of the value of clean water. Policies include eco-friendly detergents, a native plant garden and a towel re-use program. The management also offers discounts to hybrid drivers. The library is conscientiously stocked with the latest eco-education books and videos.

Food is bought from local organic growers and guests are always welcome to learn more about the garden, the local arts or even the protection of the beautiful lake through a number of projects including a regular lake clean-up.

Lookout Point Lakeside Inn has been awarded the Eco Hotels of the World rating of 4 stars.

Address:
104 Lookout Circle,
Hot Springs,
Arkansas,
USA.

Telephone:
501-525-6155

Website:
www.lookoutpointinn.com

E-mail:
innkeeper@lookoutpointinn.com

The Banyan Resort

The Banyan Resort is conveniently located in Old Town, Key West and is the ideal tropical oasis for a visit to this island paradise. Float the day away in either of the two swimming pools, unwind in the outdoor Jacuzzi or delve into a book on your private verandah. Stroll through the extensive gardens, watch the butterflies dance about the flora and spend some time beneath the ever-changing arms of one of the magical Banyan Trees.

You will find chairs and benches perfectly placed throughout the garden paths, often a sparkling fountain at this historic Key West Resort. The Tiki Bar, tucked among over 200 varieties of impressive flora and fauna, serves excellent food and frosty libations daily.Each suite in this tropical, historic resort has all the comforts of home including a full kitchen complete with the amenities necessary to make your island escape a relaxing experience. Rooms are bright and airy with ceiling fans, air conditioning, cable TV and verandahs overlooking the luxurious grounds. Floor plans range from fully-equipped studios to one- or two-bedroom suites complete with coffee maker, microwave and everything you need to prepare a meal at your leisure

Rooms:
38 suites -
(5 Studio,
28 One-Bedroom
5 Two-Bedroom)

Ave. Rates:
From $200-$260
for Studios,
$235-$310 for
One-Bedrooms
$310-$410 for
Two-Bedrooms.
(Special Events
can be higher)

Facilities on-site
Free Wi-Fi Hotspot
Bicycle Rentals
Scooter & Electric
Car Rentals,
2 Swimming Pool
- temperature
controlled by
solar-collector
Outdoor spa Jac
Poolside Tiki Ba
Gas Grills for
Guest use, Gue
Laundry Faciliti

T he Banyan Resort takes energy-efficiency seriously and solar power provides most of the energy for lights and pool heating.

The staff are aware of the Resort's green credentials and check regularly so that energy isn't wasted by lighting or cooling unoccupied rooms. Guests are reminded of their role in conservation through a towel and linen re-use program and written communication in their rooms.

Recycling is also carried out throughout the property and slightly used items donated. Most importantly Banyan Resort does a huge amount of work in the local area trying to persuade other hotels to become environmentally aware and encouraging guests to visit the reef and enjoy the local waters in a bid to showcase the area they work so hard to protect.

The Banyan Resort has been awarded the highest Eco Hotels of the World rating of 5 stars.

Address:
323 Whitehead Street,
Key West,
Florida
33040
USA

Telephone:
(305) 296-7786
Toll Free: (866) 371-9222

Website:
www.thebanyanresort.com

E-mail:
reservations@thebanyanresort.com

The DeSoto Oceanview Inn

Here at DeSoto Inns you can re-discover simple pleasures surrounded by lush gardens and azure seas. Built in 1962, this carefully restored and well-maintained Inn features cosy studios and spacious suites along a bougainvillea-shaded verandah. Guests can grab a complimentary beach chair and towel and enjoy sandy beaches at their doorstep. Here you can fish, swim, snorkel, or just kick back with a good book, and for the more energetic there are always free bicycles on site to explore the neighbourhood.

If you want to see and learn more about nature the location is perfect. DeSoto is on a barrier island in the middle of the South's largest mangrove preserve. The neighbouring Anne Kolb Nature Center provides a glimpse into Florida's eco-system, offering kayaking, boat tours and hiking for free or at nominal prices. The Everglade is only minutes away, where you can see the endangered Florida panther and alligators sunning themselves along your path to this spectacular destination.

Rooms: 9

Ave. Rates:
On Request

Activities:
Free bikes
Florida beach
Swimming
Surfing

★★★★

Since 1999, DeSoto Inns has identified and implemented energy saving practices including reduced linen services, full lighting conversion, energy saving hvac (heating, ventilation and air conditioning) and appliances, plus programs to reduce use of energy by staff and guests alike.

The gardens at the Inn are xeriscape (ecologically sound) in compliance with Florida recognition programs and lawn areas have been reduced by one third to reduce grey water consumption. In the newest property there is only Florida native landscaping which requires no supplementary water at all. Disposal has been thought through, and guests are provided with recycling receptacles while staff undertake separation and recycling. The Inn is proud of having been eco-conservative long before it became as important as it is now.

The Inn's latest promotion, 'It's Not Easy Being Green', featuring Kermit the Frog, is a huge success and aims to make eco-friendly activities available to guests. Everything spreads the word. From local art to produce, the property is committed to buying local. The management is involved in political activities including protection of the Barrier Island community, encouraging the use of public transport, bicycles (free to all guests) and programs and activities that feature the natural wonders of the area. The DeSoto Oceanview Inn has been awarded the Eco Hotels of the World rating of 4 stars.

Address:
315 Desoto Street,
Hollywood,
Florida,
33019.

Telephone:
800 686 4809
954 923 7210

Website:
www.thedesoto.com

E-mail:
thedesoto@gmail.com

The Seaport Hotel

The independently owned Seaport distinguishes itself as a deluxe hotel, meeting, exhibition, and function facility located amongst historic seaside attractions. With swift access to Logan Airport and Boston's downtown, the Hotel features a full service health club, gourmet cuisine, and wi-fi; it's also service inclusive.

Seaport has created Seaport Saves, a groundbreaking environmental program dedicated to increasing sustainability and conservation throughout all aspects of the organization. This philosophy allows the hotel to source and execute innovative improvements in an environmentally responsible way.

Guests, team members, and vendors are encouraged to practice an environmentally sensitive lifestyle as well. Seaport believes it is possible to coexist in a delicate balance with the natural world while providing world class service in a luxurious setting.

Rooms: 426

Great for Business Use

Conference centre, gym, Spa, pool, bar, restaurant

★★★★

In 2008, Seaport bought enough renewable energy credits to offset the electricity used to power all 426 guest rooms, thirteen floors, and four elevators for the entire year. Seaport employs a capacitor bank to assist with the load shedding of electricity. This smart meter and its associated sensors monitor multiple zones during peak energy-use periods in the hotel and reduce electricity by 10-20%

Other sophisticated technologies are at work here, from clever motion sensor lighting systems to a hotel-wide installation of energy efficient bulbs.

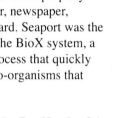

The View

Seaport recently installed an ozone system to reduce chemicals used in cleaning; this has led to a reduction in wash cycles, which along with the guest option of re-using linen has led to a savings of 585,000 gallons of water in 2007.

There is an in-room recycling program and a property-wide system for recycling white paper, newspaper, plastic, glass, aluminium, and cardboard. Seaport was the first New England location to utilise the BioX system, a revolutionary two-stage biological process that quickly eliminates organic wastes using micro-organisms that convert the waste into liquid.

The Seaport Hotel has been awarded the Eco Hotels of the World rating of 4 stars.

Address:
One Seaport Lane,
Boston,
MA,
02210,
USA.

Telephone:
1.877.SEAPORT (877.732.7678)

Website:
www.seaportboston.com

E-mail:
info@seaportboston.com

The Pool

Villa Del Faro

Villa del Faro is a hidden oasis nestled on the Sea of Cortez with acres of private beach. The Villa was created as a labour of love by artisans and architects and is an American family enterprise. It is one of the most beautiful hideaways on the East Cape of Baja Sur and is now offering very exclusive accommodations and cuisine.

There are miles of empty beach, trails into the mountains, good surfing, ocean swimming, bird watching, snorkelling, scuba-diving near-by, and whale watching from your private balcony.

Villa del Faro offers four separate Casitas powered by the sun. The Casa Alberca is a luxury lodge with a canopied king-size bed, balcony, kitchen and an elegant living room that opens right onto the large mosaic pool. Casita Tres is a lovely suite that comes with two private patios and its own outdoor living room with spectacular ocean views. Casita Dos, with a north and a south suite, is a separate house whose suites share outdoor living space and ocean views. The charming rustic Stone Beach Cottage sits right in the middle of its own deserted private beach.

Rooms:
5 Suites

Ave. Rates:
From $140 p.n
to $525 p.n.
(The entire
casa Alberca)

Facilities:
60 foot pool,
Guest dining
room and Bar,
Secluded beac
Grills and BBQ

Activities:
Surfing, Ocea
swimming,
Snorkeling,
Fishing, Divin
Horseback rid
and more...

The Villa del Faro is entirely off the grid. Each lodge is powered by solar power with a back-up generator is available for emergencies and to ensure total guest comfort.

The ecological beauty of the area is second to none. Although, as you watch the ocean lap against the desert, you can easily forget that water conservation is a top priority here, you may also fail to notice a recycling system that means the area remains uncontaminated.

Of course the emphasis is on guest relaxation but as you begin to understand the location and its limited resources you will no doubt feel proud to be supporting local conservation. Villa del Faro was doing things the green way long before most people thought it important.

Villa del Faro has been awarded the highest Eco Hotels of the World rating of 5 stars.

Address:
64 Camino Costero de La Ribera
San Jose del Cabo
Mexico

Telephone:
none

Website:
www.villadelfaro.net

E-mail:
rental@villadelfaro.net

About the Author

Alex Conti was born in Italy. Having lived in the Canary Islands and England, where he received his Masters Degree from the University of Manchester, he went on to live in France where he spends his time travelling and writing.

His travel experiences and love for the environment motivated the creation of this book, his first travel guide. He is a Fellow of the Royal Geographical Society, a keen sailor, a reasonable cyclist and a proponent of the view that tourism can probably solve all of the world's problems.

Acknowledgements

To My Friends and Family,

Few people realise the incredible effort that goes into creating even the simplest of books. With this interminable struggle, comes the search for friends and family willing and able to give a helping hand despite the absence of economic rewards. With this book, I have been lucky to find a whole network of people (we now jokingly call the 'European Free-labour Group') who willingly gave their spare time in the pursuit of this worthwhile and exciting project. To everyone involved, my sincerest appreciation and admiration, without all of you this book would not have been possible and for that I am extremely grateful.

To Natalie,
Everything I do is simply the creative outcome of your patience and support. Thank you for generously sharing me with "Eco Hotels of the World"

Research
Trevor Pittendreigh

Cover Photo
Sascha Burkard

Sales
Kate Baker

Mapping
Alex Cubbin

Proof Reading
Natalie Kunert

Important Notice:

The world of tourism is fast changing so please ensure you always confirm prices, facilities, travel facts and general information when you are planning your trip. We cannot be deemed responsible for any involuntary errors or omissions printed herein. We have done our very best to ensure the information contained within this guide is accurate and dependable. However, we cannot accept any responsibility for any loss, injury or inconvenience resulting from the use of information contained in this guide

Alphabetical Property Index